DAVID NAYLOR AND JOAN DILLON

AMERICAN THEATERS

Performance Halls of the Nineteenth Century

FOREWORD BY JULIE HARRIS

Preservation Press

John Wiley & Sons, Inc.

NEW YORK · CHICHESTER · WEINHEIM · TORONTO · SINGAPORE · BRISBANE

This text is printed on acid-free paper.

This publication is designed to provide accurate and authoritative information in regard to the subject matter covered. It is sold with the understanding that the publisher is not engaged in rendering legal, accounting, or other professional services. If legal advice or other expert assistance is required, the services of a competent professional person should be sought.

LIBRARY OF CONGRESS CATALOGING-IN-PUBLICATION DATA

Naylor, David, 1955–
    American theaters : performance halls of the nineteenth century / David Naylor and Joan Dillon ; foreword by Julie Harris.
        p.   cm.
    Includes index.
    ISBN 0-471-14393-6 (cloth : alk. paper)
    1. Theaters—United States—History—19th century. 2. Theater architecture—United States. 3. Architecture, Modern—19th century— United States. I. Dillon, Joan, 1925–   . II. Title.
NA6830.D56   1997
725′.822′097309034—dc20   96-43764

Printed in the United States of America

10 9 8 7 6 5 4 3 2 1

Designed by Robert L. Wiser, Archetype Press, Inc., Washington, D.C.

Photograph on page 1:
Belfast Opera House (1866),
Belfast, Maine.

PROJECT SPONSORS

This book was made possible in large part through the help and support of the officers, members, and the staff of the League of Historic American Theatres (LHAT).

LHAT and the authors express their gratitude to the following people who provided funds for the photodocumentation project:

Mr. and Mrs. Frank Weil
Mr. and Mrs. Morton Sosland
Mr. and Mrs. George Dillon

THIS BOOK IS DEDICATED TO THE MEMORY OF

Gene Chesley

FRIEND AND FOUNDER
OF THE
LEAGUE OF HISTORIC AMERICAN THEATRES

Contents

Symphony Hall
(1899), Allentown,
Pennsylvania.

An Actor's Foreword to the American Theater

As I look through pictures of these older theaters, they naturally evoke certain thoughts and memories. As an actor, I will play anywhere—warm, cold, in a garage, wherever. But these nineteenth-century theaters are special. These buildings make me want to get close to them, feel them, experience them. Theatre is always best when the auditorium has a certain welcoming feeling. The finest American theaters have a quality not unlike the older opera houses of Italy, as at La Scala in Milan or at the Teatro Rossini, where, standing on the empty stage, looking around, the theater seems to say, "Come to me." These are places for magic.

These buildings have their ghosts, too. When I visited the Tabor Opera House in Leadville, Colorado, I felt there were ghosts present. They belonged to the actors and singers whose voices have seeped into the atmosphere. I have had the good fortune to perform in other Colorado theaters as well—the Wheeler Opera House in Aspen, the Central City Opera House, and the old Elitch Theatre, though the last was a bit of a shock at that time. I found myself performing inside a building right next to a roller coaster. I heard it all the time. And then, with a tin roof, when it rained . . .

But a theater doesn't have to be old to be special. When I did *The Belle of Amherst* at the Guthrie Theater in Minneapolis, it was extraordinary. I felt as if the audience at this modern theater were right there in my mind. What is most critical to me is that the theatre is a thing of the voice; to hear the word is the reason people go to the theatre. And it is in this realm that the older buildings excel. The people who built theaters then knew how to promote sound, in such a way that audiences remembered how to listen.

As for favorites among these places, it is impossible to name just one. Having only visited previously, I'd love to play Ford's Theatre in Washington, D.C. Then there's that little opera house in Lexington, Kentucky, where we did both *The Belle of Amherst* and *Lucifer's Child*. Such places are wonderfully suited to live performance. From the actor's standpoint, their stages enable us to draw the audience into the play. I will always be in favor of preserving these buildings. I hope we can retain this sort of theater where the possibility for dramatic magic is always present.

JULIE HARRIS

8

A Manager's Foreword to the American Theater

I t was early in my tenure (currently nearing thirty years) here at the Goodspeed Opera House when the core group of what was to become the League of Historic American Theatres (LHAT) first met. Following our first formal gathering, held in 1977 at Thrall's Opera House in New Harmony, Indiana, the League coalesced. I was fortunate to be named its first president. We were a small but dedicated group, and of those involved in the establishment of LHAT, Gene Chesley stands out as the true historian and the one most interested in documenting the existence of our theaters. The rest of us were more interested in conducting dialogues among ourselves and discovering other theaters that might be restored and given a useful new life. In today's parlance, we were networking. But from the start, there has always been the dual purpose of documenting the past and restoring for the future. Our efforts are spent to preserve both the history of these theaters, as written record, and the buildings, in direct nuts-and-bolts fashion.

This book is in keeping with the twin goals of the League. In it are both general and specific histories, in every case enlivened by an illustration of how these theaters have variously suffered and thrived, and continue to do so as times have changed. Not one of these older venues looks or operates exactly as it did in the nineteenth century. We must appreciate each not only for its historic value but also for its contemporary use. Adaptive use gives life to a static form of sculpture (architecture), which vibrates with the essence of the old and the new. So, with one eye to the past and one to the future, the League and its kindred organizations must continue this dual-track mission. And we should all applaud the work behind this book and, likewise, the tenacity of the various individuals and institutions involved in the renovation and reactivation of historic theaters. Thanks to such efforts, these buildings remain living contributors to the communities that have preserved them.

MICHAEL P. PRICE

Goodspeed Opera House
(1877), East Haddam,
Connecticut.

Introduction: "An Opera House by Any Name"

During the years spent developing this book, we faced all sorts of decisions about which buildings to include and, then, how best to present them. Certain ground rules were established as we went along. We agreed that all inclusions must be American theaters opened before the end of 1900, be currently in use and open to the public. We then proceeded—at times with glee—to break every one of our rules.

In the face of such glorious spectacles as the Haskell Opera House in Derby Line, Vermont, we found ourselves powerless to hold the line on our restrictions. This particular latecomer to the Victorian era breaks *all* the rules. The Haskell, which combines a library and a performance hall under one roof, was built in 1903–04 and currently sits empty, closed indefinitely until certain perplexing aspects of fire safety and preservation are resolved. Moreover, this is not a wholly American theater, as the building obliquely straddles the U.S.-Canadian border. Still, it must be recognized that the Haskell and a few other early twentieth-century theaters are Victorian in spirit, if not precisely in age. A few reconstructed theaters demanded some consideration, too, particularly the Dock Street Theatre in Charleston, South Carolina, as a 1937 version of a postulated 1736 interior. Additional exceptions were made for older buildings that were converted for theatrical uses in the early or even mid-twentieth century, such as the Barter Theater in Abingdon, Virginia. Finally, some shuttered but still noteworthy performance spaces were included as long as someone or some organization was found to be working toward a reopening.

To assemble a pool of candidates for inclusion, more than one thousand five hundred leads on theaters were pursued by phone and by postcard, with follow-up questionnaires sent to more than one thousand venues. Eventually, one or both of us paid a call to a combined total of more than two hundred fifty sites, nearly always welcomed at the doors (though we must confess to a small number of unscheduled, "self-guided" tours). The fruits of our labors not only resulted in this book and the making of some solid friendships but also unearthed a few "facts" likely to interest future theater historians: more than one-quarter of these halls have "perfect" acoustics, about a third possess "unique" horseshoe balconies, and at least four are the "oldest" in the United States, two in "continuous operation."

It is easy to make fun of such claims but, at the same time, these statements are a testament to the pride that people still feel in these older-model showplaces. Perhaps worn, but not worn-out, these nineteenth-century theaters maintain a place in both the memories and the physical contexts of the communities that continue to support them. This show of unflagging pride is what informed, at least in part, our decisions as to exactly what we would call these places. After all, which should be known as an opera house, or even a grand opera house? Despite various published attempts to codify such matters, we chose to hold to a case-by-case attitude best described as

The founders of the Chautauqua Auditorium (1898) and Chautauqua Park in Boulder, Colorado, defined their mission as "the drawing together of people for discussion, entertainment, and recreation." (Carnegie Branch Library for Local History, Boulder Historical Society)

laissez faire. For us, "An opera house by any name" means that each place can be called whatever its community wishes, whether it produces grand opera or Grand Funk. This seemed most appropriate because these theaters were seen by their builders and their patrons as markers of cultural pride. Even if opera was the *last* thing that townspeople would expect to see on their local stage, this would not diminish in the slightest the significance they attached to their theater building. For many, the title "opera house" best expressed the measure of that significance.

Adopting this egalitarian attitude toward nomenclature in no way simplified our job of dividing the surviving nineteenth-century theaters into manageable groups for presentation. What ultimately made most sense was something of a hybrid approach. We broke down our list of venues into "theater genres," developed with an eye first to the regions of the country where certain types of buildings with related spatial configurations had evolved. The secondary consideration involved the kinds of performances most typically presented at a given theater. Too often, though, the attempt to determine a single prevalent use, from over a century or more of productions, proved a meaningless task. We simply did our best to make sense, in almost narrative fashion, of the rich variety of performance spaces constructed during the nineteenth century in America.

Through all our ruminations, there was one point upon which our resolution never wavered. It concerned an apparently simple matter of spelling. Our position is that, while we may go to see a *theatre* performance, we watch it in a *theater* building. Of course, this building may be known as an opera house, or a music hall, or a chautauqua. We have done our utmost to respect the preferred spellings of the performance halls included, when we refer to each by name. Every one is a unique creation, and can be called by any name. Collectively, by us, they will always be known as *theaters*, and be no less sweet for that.

The American Performance Hall through
HISTORY

Early American Theater Buildings

THE THEATERS BUILT IN NINETEENTH-CENTURY AMERICA's cities and towns were the chief repositories of their communities' cultural hopes and dreams. Each town's aspirations to deserve its spot on the map were caught up with the scale and grandeur of their public buildings, and theaters often were the most prominent emblem of local pride. Even the most ramshackle opera house carried a heavy symbolic load. Its mere existence signified that the people who built it, after traveling so far to settle this new country, were here to stay, no matter how fragile each fresh settlement might appear. The patrons of each newly built entertainment venue along the fringes of nineteenth-century America, were determined to be as prosperous and, eventually, as culturally sophisticated as anyone else, in this country or in Europe or Asia.

By the time the United States had gained independence in the late eighteenth century, a small assortment of theaters throughout the country had already been built. The town of Williamsburg, Virginia, counted a playhouse among its public structures in the early 1700s. The major colonial cities of Boston and New York, Philadelphia, and Charleston, South Carolina, were each home to a variety of performance halls. According to the book *Philadelphia Theaters*, by Irvin R. Glazer, that city was head and shoulders above the others on this score: "Philadelphia's preeminence as a theatrical center lasted until 1830, after which New York City became the entertainment capital." The book notes that among the earliest post-colonial theaters in America was the first of a number of Philadelphia venues (all razed) to bear the name of the Chestnut Street Theatre, opened in 1794. The layout of this building was inspired by that of a theater in Bath, England. Architect Henry Latrobe, himself English-born, gave the original Chestnut Street Theatre a new façade in 1805.

The involvement of Latrobe in refashioning this theater served as an indication of the willingness shown by the first professional architects working in the new United States to take on theatrical commissions. Such readiness could not be taken for granted, particularly in a city such as Philadelphia, where the social and clerical elite worked together to elevate the public's moral standards, a goal that theaters and theatrical performers were often perceived by these groups as undermining. Nonetheless, another prominent Philadelphia-based architect, John Haviland, did not shy away from theater design. The new front he constructed in 1828 for the Walnut Street Theatre (1809) is among his many surviving landmark buildings. This street façade by Haviland

A sample of the carved woodwork decorating the Norfolk Opera House (1883) in Norfolk, Connecticut.

14

is the principal link to the past for this surviving venue, whose interior was altered severely in the twentieth century. Near Boston, another prominent early nineteenth-century architect, Asher Benjamin, inadvertently produced a theater in Warrenton, Massachusetts. A church he designed in 1843 came to be used as the Charles Playhouse.

For the most part, however, the designing of this country's early theaters was the province of local builders, not theater specialists. Thus, the relative architectural qualities of these venues were largely dependent on the skills of the workers that were available, a situation very different from that where longstanding crafts traditions produced the grand concert halls of Europe in the 1700s and 1800s. The most spectacular of these, built in the eighteenth century, included Italy's Teatro alla Scala (1778) in Milan, by Giuseppe Piermarini, and Jacques Ange Gabriel's Opera (1770) at Versailles in France. Such opulent showplaces might just as well have been built on the moon for all the early American theater builders knew about their appearances. It would take another century before the first photographic images of such European halls would be published widely in the United States. The Philadelphia Academy of Music, completed to the designs of architects LeBrun & Runge in 1857, shows an indebtedness to La Scala and to comparable Italian halls of the period such as the Teatro Comunale in Ferrara. The multitiered opera houses epitomized by these theaters were relatively rare in the United States, although they were more popular elsewhere in the New World, as inside the Teatro Colon in Buenos Aires, Argentina.

More significant to the evolution of theater design in North America were radical developments in interior layout planning that took place in eighteenth-century France. In traditional European plans, the prime seats in the tiers of opera boxes formed a ring around a low central space, the pit or parterre, which was the domain of the more raucous, less well-to-do classes. Among the tiers, only the upper ring tucked just under the ceiling was regarded as unsuitable to finer tastes, and thus was often occupied by the servants of any royalty or aristocrats in attendance. This arrangement was altered most notably by French architect Claude-Nicolas Ledoux for his theater at Besançon (1784). Inside its auditorium, the premier seats were located along the raked main floor. Above a dress circle partitioned only by low walls, the upper seating areas formed a simple amphitheater, with a semicircular colonnade set behind the topmost gallery seats. Ledoux's subversion of the conventional seating pattern of his era provided the basic prototype for the interior configuration that remains most popular worldwide to this day.

In the United States during the nineteenth century, theater configurations often found a middle ground between the conventional opera house plans and the innovative scheme of Ledoux. Such was the case inside New York City's Metropolitan Opera House, opened in 1893 and razed long ago. Although seats on the main floor must have been quite comfortable, they were not regarded as the choice tickets they would be on the Broadway of today, because the social affairs and intrigues of the city's elite were able to be conducted clandestinely in the private boxes of the Metropolitan. This grand dame of New York theaters served as the namesake, if not an exact model, for numerous smaller theaters around the country, including the Metropolitan Theatre (1899) in Iowa Falls, Iowa. More often than not, however, American theater builders chose to follow the patterns for seating established by Ledoux at Besançon.

Toward the end of the nineteenth century, arts patrons in the Midwest and the western regions of the country began to call upon the newly emerging class of architects whose practices typically involved some theater design. Among the best known and most talented firms was the Chicago partnership of Dankmar Adler and Louis Sullivan. While their practice was not devoted to theater design, the two architects had already produced the Academy of Music (1882, razed) in Kalamazoo, Michigan, and rebuilt Chicago's McVicker's Theatre in 1885, when the commission to build the Midwest's largest venue came their way the following year: the landmark Auditorium Building (1889), which opened at the southeast corner of the Chicago Loop. While working on the Auditorium Building, Adler & Sullivan had received a letter from the Opera House Association of Pueblo, Colorado, which had lost its pride and joy, the DeRemer Opera House, to fire in May 1888. Pueblo's civic leaders read published accounts of the Auditorium Theater under construction, and decided to contact the architects about building a replacement for their destroyed showplace. One, possibly both, of the architects traveled to Pueblo to oversee the building of a new opera house block. Louis Sullivan must have visited at least once, considering his recorded comments: "The climate of Colorado is dry and warm, the atmosphere is glaring, the air very clear."

The view from the stage at the Philadelphia Academy of Music (1857) shows the strong kinship to the best of the Old World opera houses.

The exterior cladding of the Pueblo Opera House Block (1890) was built of reddish Manitou stone, massed to provide deep recesses along its arcaded sides and in the loggia of the observatory tower. This aspect of the design was Sullivan's response to the site of the opera house, in keeping with his reported comment that "a building should be adapted to the climate of the locality in which it is built." Another sentiment, attributed to Sullivan in the local newspaper, makes him seem somewhat condescending about the Pueblo block: "The design of the building, in its general conception and handling, is somewhat in advance of the present practice in your section of the country."

In any event, the citizens of Pueblo were thrilled with their new opera house, with its grand entry arches of carved stone and gilded interior. Those present opening night dressed in such finery that the front-page newspaper descriptions of the ladies in attendance rivaled the accounts of the decor of the new theater and the opening-night performances. In subsequent decades the opera house maintained its place as the revered center of social life in Pueblo, but sadly, fire claimed the building in the early morning hours of February 28, 1922. Despite every effort of the local firefighters, working in a subzero winter storm, the opera house was gutted to its stone walls.

It was believed that the fire began in the wooden ballroom above the theater auditorium. Late-night revelers had already left the building, so no one was injured in the Pueblo fire, but fatalities were often part of similar stories elsewhere. Pueblo's tragedy was all too familiar to the nineteenth-century theater scene. Many opera houses of the day were constructed principally of wood and prior to the use of fully electrified lighting systems, pioneered in the big-city halls such as the Auditorium Theater, the candles and gas jets used to illuminate performances put the buildings in constant jeopardy. The fire that destroyed the Richmond Theater in Virginia, on the day after Christmas in 1811, resulted in the deaths of seventy-one patrons. The worst theater fire in American history was the infamous blaze that leveled Chicago's Iroquois Theater in December 1903. Although advertised as fireproof, the theater's stage apparently had a faulty fire curtain and, because the exit doors had been chained shut, the disaster resulted in 581 deaths. Criminal prosecutions followed. Since then, precautionary

measures and safety investigations instituted at old and new theaters nationwide have helped to prevent theater fires of even approximately comparable magnitude.

By the turn of the century, the design and construction of theaters had become the province of architects who specialized in these buildings. Most prolific among these were John Bailey McElfatrick and his sons John Morgan and William. McElfatrick & Sons built their first theater in 1855 not far from the firm's office in St. Louis, Missouri. Relocated to New York in 1884, the partnership went on to produce more than sixty theaters in the city's five boroughs. The total number of theaters nationwide built by the McElfatricks has been estimated to be as many as two hundred different designs.

Diversity was a trademark of nineteenth-century American theaters on the whole in those years. There was no clearinghouse, no publication devoted to theater design, as there would be in the twentieth-century era of movie palaces. Until certain illustrated journals did come into broad circulation toward the end of the 1800s, theater builders outside the major cities were left to their own devices. Although, presumably, the basic principles of this realm of design would have been apparent to any builder who had ever attended a theatre performance, exactly how a new American theater should look or be configured remained open to interpretation. Such a free hand, relative to the more formalized practices in Europe, resulted in a few architectural atrocities among the new venues in America, however functional they may have been. Despite any architectural shortcomings, theaters in the rural towns of the East and the mining towns of the West played major roles in the lives of the local inhabitants. For every ornamental faux pas committed in these theaters, a dozen decorative and technical innovations were produced. The result, even in an abbreviated list of only the surviving nineteenth-century American theaters, is an assortment of buildings as entrancing and wonderful as any of the acts they showcased. Artists and architects in the late nineteenth century worked to establish a cultural identity unique to America. Rarely was it expressed more successfully than in the concert halls and opera houses of the day.

Above: Scaled down from its New York City namesake, the Metropolitan (1899) in Iowa Falls, Iowa, still puts up an impressive front.

Opposite: This 1893 sketch of the original Metropolitan Opera House in New York City provides a glimpse of how the cream of Manhattan society spent their evenings on the town.

The Pueblo Opera House Block (1890) was designed by Adler & Sullivan to stand the test of time, but this Colorado showplace was felled by fire in 1922. (Both courtesy of Pueblo County Historical Society; opposite photograph also courtesy of Elsie Hendrix)

Backstage in the 1800s

THE BACKSTAGES OF MOST THEATERS BUILT IN THE NINETEENTH century resembled more than anything else the decks of the great sailing ships of the era. Hemp ropes, used to raise and lower stage scenery, were locked in position by belaying pins along a wooden pin rail. Winchlike mechanisms, known as windlasses, were found both above the grids spanning the stages and below stage level. These were used primarily to help adjust the rope lines. Sandbags used as counterweights in these systems also contributed to the nautical appearance of a typical backstage.

Nineteenth-century stage sets were mostly a continuation of the so-called wing and drop type developed earlier, and still in use in many older theaters today. The drops were sheets of canvas that measured only a few feet, or as wide as the full stage opening, their fronts painted to match the settings of the scenes to be played. Each drop could be raised or rolled up to reveal other scenes hung in succession. Wing scenery, so named for its location at the side wings of the stage, was also made of painted canvas stretched over lightweight wooden frames. These frames were guided onstage at the appropriate moments in specially built grooves or tracks. Less prosperous theaters had only meager amounts of scenery; thriving operations had a dozen sets or more. A typical collection might include a bosky forest, a formal garden, a street scene, and various interiors, both elaborate and plain.

The method most often used for painting scenery in the nineteenth century began by hanging a blank canvas against the back wall of a stage. Scene painters then raised or lowered themselves along the face of the canvas on moveable bridges suspended on ropes, often wrapped around the large windlasses above the stage grid. The Folly Theater (1900) in Kansas City, Missouri, still has a windlass, six feet in diameter, once used for this purpose. The Folly's moveable bridge is gone, however, sacrificed in exchange for precious backstage space during renovation work in 1975.

As attempts were made in the 1800s to develop a greater sense of realism in stage productions, scenery and costumes were designed to be more historically accurate. Full landscape scenes replaced simple garden settings on those occasions that called for grander vistas. More backstage space was allocated to scenery, props, and dressing areas. Each dramatic production was run like a tight ship. Over the course of the century, there was a sharp upturn in the number of shows that traveled from town to town, particularly after the railroads were in place by midcentury. Many touring productions brought

Painted scenery credited
to Maxfield Parrish in the
1920s still hangs inside the
Plainfield Town Hall (1798)
in New Hampshire.

their own costumes and scenery with them, a practice that resulted in some interesting architectural innovations. Stage flats (scenery panels) had to be standardized in size, their dimensions matching those of the doors on railway boxcars. Subsequently, stage doors through which scenery was brought backstage had to be sized to match as well. Scenery handling was made especially easy in Abilene, Kansas, where the stage doors for the Plaza Theater (1879) opened right beside the railroad tracks. By the end of the nineteenth century, there were at least five hundred theater companies touring the nation, although some estimates double that number.

For all the industrial advances that took place in the nineteenth century, most backstage machinery had not been significantly improved since the 1700s—and earlier. Only in the 1890s, with fully integrated electric lighting, did major changes begin to occur. Candlepower had only given way to gas lamps in the early decades of the century. Traditionally, candles had been mounted on chandeliers in the upper reaches inside the theaters, with more on brackets around the walls. Buckets of water were placed at strategic locations around the theater, in case of fire. It was the sole task of one stagehand, the "snuff boy," to trim and tend all the candles, even if it meant going on stage during a performance.

Prior to the introduction of gas lighting, oil lamps were tried in place of candles, but patrons often complained of the strong smell. Theater managers were left to choose between dripping wax or foul odors as the price for lighting their shows. Records suggest that Philadelphia's Chestnut Street Theatre (1816) was the first performance hall to be lit entirely by gas.

Improvements to gas lighting were made steadily throughout the century. The early Argaud burners were replaced by the 1890s with Welsbach burners, known for producing a more even, steady white glow. Limelight, so closely associated with theatrical performances, was produced by a gas flame from a blowpipe, its radiance concentrated by a lens. This allowed for a "spotlight" effect that could be directed to follow an actor around the stage for the duration of an entire scene. As one legend has it, Sarah Bernhardt had a stagehand fully equipped and suspended above stage in a basket to follow her about with limelight through an entire production of *Camille*.

The viability of electrical systems, first introduced in 1879, brought about safer lighting systems. However, the earliest electric arc lamps brought their own problems: a high level of noise in operation and the relative coldness of the light quality compared with candles or gas lamps. These problems were resolved in the twentieth century by the development of incandescent spotlights.

Other innovations in the nineteenth century impacted the practices of stage design. The Booth Theater (1869; razed) in New York City, with its seventy-six-foot-high stagehouse, brought an alternative to the old wing and drop system. Drops could now be flown up above the stage opening, out of sight of the audience. The newly uncluttered wing areas meant more room for other props and greater freedom of movement for the actors.

Another traditional device, the trapdoor, was updated around this time. These doors of various sizes, cut into stage floors, enabled such illusions as the sudden appearance of a "ghost" or the disappearance of a ship sinking at sea. Trapdoors had been used for centuries, but those new in the late nineteenth century were often hydraulically powered and facilitated the use of more massive stage sets. Until electricity became

This Chinese windlass is a prize possession of the Folly Theater (1900) in Kansas City, Missouri. (Folly Theater)

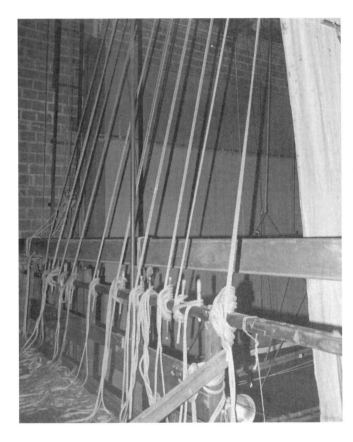

Thalian Hall (1858) in Wilmington, North Carolina, has managed to retain many of its nineteenth-century backstage features, including its pin rail, a rain machine, and a windlass. (Thalian Hall Archives Collection)

the norm, hydraulic stage elements and revolving stages popular in the latter half of the century were powered by counterweights.

Popular new plays of that period required stage designers to constantly expand their repertoire of special theatrical effects. A standard array of contraptions included snow cradles, rumble carts, bull roarers, crash machines, and mechanical contrivances to simulate wind or rain. To make a rain machine, a rotating barrel drum with a handle attached was laid on its side, and filled with dried beans, which, when the barrel revolved, created the sound of a soft rain; marbles and buckshot were used to simulate a heavy storm. Another drum, turned rapidly under a fixed sheet of canvas, mimicked the sound of wind. A snow cradle was constructed by stretching fabric between two battens, which resembled a swing seat hanging high above the stage. The "cradle" was filled with paper confetti, which, on cue, was released to flutter slowly to the floor as the battens were jerked back and forth by stagehands positioned up on the catwalks.

If it was noise rather than weather that was needed, nothing beat the grunts and squeaks of the bull roarers. To create this special noisemaker, one end of a metal can was removed, and a cord was threaded through a hole in the other end. A stagehand held the cord taut and rubbed it with a resined cloth to produce the desired sounds. Crash machines featured rotating drums set beneath a row of hardwood slats. As a drum was turned, pegs along its sides raised and released each slat in turn, which then snapped back against the drum to make the crashing noises.

Rumble carts, on the other hand, were mobile boxes filled with weights and set on lug wheels. As a cart was rolled around backstage, it variously sounded like the passing of a heavy vehicle or distant thunder. The latter effect was best achieved by a custom-built device known as a thunder run or thunder roll. One or more wooden troughs were attached to a backstage wall in a switchback pattern. Cannonballs, housed in a rabbit hutch at the top of the runs, were then dropped, one after the other, into the troughs where they rumbled with a sound like thunder. Thalian Hall (1858) in Wilmington, North Carolina, still uses its old run, complete with nineteenth-century cannonballs.

Another device commonly used to make thunder was a sheet of iron fastened at its top to wooden boards. These sheets, when shaken, resounded in great claps of "thunder." The original sheet was constructed in 1708 by John Dennis, who so jealously guarded his invention that, reportedly, he often accused others of "stealing his thunder."

Another special effect, which was needed to stage the chariot race for productions of *Ben Hur* or the scene in *Uncle Tom's Cabin* where dogs chase little Eva across the ice, was created by setting a treadmill into the stage floor. The animals for these stunts were trained to slow down and get off the apparatus at the right moment. Another method used to suggest movement was the panorama strip scene. A continuous backdrop painted on a long roll of canvas was unwound to pass from one side of the stage to the other, and wrapped around a spool at the opposite side. The stage lights were dimmed for these scenes, to enhance the impression of apparent motion on stage.

Some stages in nineteenth-century halls were raked on a slight incline rising from front to back, in order to allow patrons in the back rows a better view of the performances. A small number of flat-floored halls had a different way of dealing with audience sightlines. More common in New England than elsewhere, a mechanism was devised that enabled the main floor of an auditorium to change from a level to a raked position. The front row of seats could be lowered as much as a few feet. In some cases, only the front half of the

A highlight of Thalian Hall's backstage sound-effects devices is a cannonball-operated thunder roll. The wooden troughs of the thunder roll cross, switchback-fashion, along one wall of the stagehouse. (Thalian Hall Archives Collection)

This illustration depicts one
way that stage treadmills were
put into service in French
theaters. (Courtesy of Harvard
Theatre Collection)

Stage curtains such as this one hanging inside Piper's Opera House (1885) in Virginia City, Nevada, were a standard feature in small-town theaters well into the 1900s. (LHAT)

seating was lowered, by means of an axis located in the middle of the hall. A fully tilting floor was more typical, with some theaters requiring two sets of entry doors as a result. The usual hoisting mechanism was powered by jack screws or hydraulics located in the theater basements, which lowered and raised the floor by means of leather belts or metal screws; some systems were worked by hand and others by mechanized systems. The front half of the floor of the St. George (Utah) Social Hall (1864) was tilted by a large crank and cog wheels, on which leather straps wound and unwound in the process. Lowering the floor meant the stage was four feet high above the front-row seats. Wooden slats were pegged into place in the floor to keep the chairs from sliding forward. Of all the convertible theaters built in the nineteenth century, the St. George hall is the only one known to have its hoisting mechanism still in place, although it is no longer operable.

All of these wondrous backstage, above-stage, and below-stage devices were, of course, most effective when the audience was unaware of their use. If, in the 1800s, backstage resembled the makeup of a ship, vast numbers of the crew—stagehands, technicians, costumers—were invisible to the "passengers." When all the effects came off without a hitch, a stage production provided smooth sailing indeed.

Survival and Revival in the Twentieth Century

THE FATE OF MOST OF THE OLDER THEATERS THAT SURVIVED into the current century has depended more on their location, size, and flexibility of use than on any architectural merits. Many nineteenth-century theaters became obsolete simply because their towns outgrew them. New forms of entertainment led to new types of theater buildings. Vaudeville and burlesque could still be staged in the largest of the older venues, but the booming movie business required a succession of bigger and glitzier theaters. Age alone took its toll on some surviving nineteenth-century halls, making these buildings far more susceptible to fire. Fire destroyed much of the original Honolulu Music Hall (1883) in early 1895. Although it was rebuilt later that year on the same site, right across from the Iolani Palace, and reopened as the Hawaiian Opera House, the second version was never as popular as its predecessor. Neither its eventual shift to movie house status nor its proximity to the royal palace was enough to save the theater from replacement by municipal buildings in 1917. The Hawaiian could not withstand the tides of redevelopment in its modern urban setting.

Given the physical dangers of older structures, economic competition, and twentieth-century America's increasing appetite for novelty in its cultural tastes, it is a wonder so many older theaters survived at all. But some enterprising opera house owners not only foresaw the threat posed by the motion picture industry, they met the challenge by accommodating the movies. Bright electric signboards were hung off classically ordered cast-iron theater façades. At more than a few older showplaces, entire interiors were revamped. Not a single feature inside the Victoria Theatre (1866) in Dayton, Ohio, remains from its past, following a 1920s remodeling into a movie palace. A few of the older theaters possessed built-in flexibility, thanks to the planning by their original architects. The Cincinnati Music Hall (1878) came equipped with a collapsible wooden floor that could be unfolded to temporarily level the main floor area. This device enabled the auditorium to serve as overflow space for the exhibition hall that occupied the northern portion of the vast Music Hall complex. The building, designed by eminent Ohioans Samuel Hannaford and Henry Proctor, was especially prized by the predominantly German population that resided in the communities surrounding the building. Yet, ultimately, the only thing that forestalled the wrecking ball from knocking on the Music Hall doors in the twentieth century was

The Folly Theater (1900) in Kansas City, Missouri, looked decrepit before local citizens brought it back to good health. (Folly Theater)

35

Opposite: The interior of
Dayton, Ohio's Victoria
Theatre (1866) lost its Victorian
decor in a movie-palace
makeover in the 1920s.

Above: The Springer Auditorium
in the Cincinnati Music Hall
(1878) doubled as an exhibition
hall, when the need arose,
by unfolding a temporary
floor over the seats. (Courtesy
of Cincinnati Music Hall)

Above: The former
Stockbridge Casino (1888) in
Massachusetts became a
playhouse in 1928, with a new
name, the Berkshire Theater.

Opposite: McKim, Mead &
White's Newport Casino
(1880) in Rhode Island made
an easy transition into the
International Tennis Hall
of Fame, but its Casino
Theatre is wasted as a storage
space for umpires' chairs
and electronic scoreboards.

the sheer immensity of the structure. This great cathedral-like mass of brick was simply too big to demolish without driving the wreckers into bankruptcy.

Prior to the founding of various architecture and theater preservation organizations, the sad fact is that the architectural pedigree of many of the older theaters was rarely a factor in whether they survived or disappeared in the early twentieth century. The situation has improved steadily since the bad old days of urban renewal in the mid-1960s, yet even with increased historical awareness, a number of older theaters by some well-known American architects sit derelict or are ill-used. Stanford White designed the Casino Theatre (1880) as part of the fabled Newport Casino complex in Rhode Island. Although most of this ensemble of buildings, by the firm of McKim, Mead & White, has found a new use as the International Tennis Hall of Fame, the theater auditorium remains a desolate space, covered in dust and used as a catchall storage bin. Another building by the firm, the former Stockbridge Casino (1888) in Massachusetts was moved to the edge of town in 1928. There it received a new lease on life, refurbished as the Berkshire Theater, a home to summer stock productions.

The cruelest reincarnation of a theater took place in California where the Sonora Opera Hall (1885) was converted first into a carpentry shop in 1899, and then, in 1911, reshaped as an automobile repair shop. The old stage and proscenium arch were left in place inside the Opera Hall Garage, but main-floor seating gave way to the principal service area, complete with oil pits. The City of Sonora finally put an end to the repairs-in-the-round, when it acquired the property in 1986 and started the hall on the road to recovery. The renovated theater reopened in 1995.

Grassroots efforts to save old buildings, including theaters, date back some years before the National Trust for Historic Preservation received its charter in 1949. In the

Above: After decades serving as an auto repair shop, the Sonora Opera Hall (1885) in California was reclaimed as a theater space by the town in 1995. (LHAT)

Opposite: On its busier days, the crowds waiting to see Ford's Theatre (1863) spill out onto the sidewalk of this popular Washington, D.C., landmark.

case of the Dock Street Theatre (1937) in Charleston, South Carolina, preservationists took action, even though there was no theater building left to restore. The first Dock Street Theatre opened February 12, 1736, in what was then known as Charles Town. The building perished in a fire just a few years after the opening. Two later theaters on the same site were also long gone when construction began to enlarge the Planter's Hotel, which had been moved to this site in 1809. By then, Dock Street had been renamed Church Street, as nearby St. Philip's Church had become the dominant building in the neighborhood. The transplanted hotel, reputed to be the initial purveyor of Planter's Punch, was spruced up in 1855, with a cast-iron balcony suspended above its street-level entrance colonnade. By the 1930s, the building was in shambles, when concerned citizens developed a plan to reconstruct the 1736 theater within the ruins of the former hotel. Efforts to produce a semblance of the original interior, under the sponsorship of the Works Progress Administration, were speculative at best. Nevertheless, the current Dock Street Theatre put on its own grand reopening on November 21, 1937. On the program was a revival of the inaugural 1736 production, *The Recruiting Officer*. The city-owned building continues in operation, overseen by the Charleston Department of Special Facilities.

Above: Scaffolding was set up to repair the southern face of the all-wood exterior of the Goodspeed Opera House (1877) in East Haddam, Connecticut, during its renovation in the 1960s. (Diane Sobolewski)

Opposite: Pew-style seating is available on the main floor inside the reconstructed Dock Street Theatre in Charleston, South Carolina (1736; reconstructed 1937).

Another theatrical reclamation project involved Ford's Theatre (1863) in Washington, D.C. Now a national shrine as the site where President Abraham Lincoln was assassinated, the theater was originally a reconstruction of an 1833-vintage church. Baltimore-based theater owner John T. Ford leased the church building in 1861, but was forced to renovate the property after fire destroyed part of the structure the following year. The new Ford's of 1863 hosted a total of four hundred and ninety-five performances, from its opening night until it closed after the President's assassination on the evening of April 14, 1865. Historical records note that assassin John Wilkes Booth, leaping to make his escape, broke his leg landing on the Ford's stage that night, after he became entangled in the decorative bunting of the presidential box.

Within the current interior, restored as a museum in 1968, American flags are permanently draped over the front of the box. The century that preceded the conversion to museum status had been less than kind to Ford's Theatre. Used after 1865 as federal offices, the interior collapsed in 1893, killing twenty-two people. Demoted thereafter to use as a storage facility, it was not until 1933, and its acquisition by the National Park Service, that the old theater was shored up and maintained until its restoration.

With so many older theaters now renovated for use as performance centers, it is easy to overlook how remarkable the first of such rescue efforts were. The Goodspeed Opera House (1877), located in East Haddam, Connecticut, benefited from a visionary salvage operation carried out in 1962. At a time when modern halls clad in concrete were becoming the rage and older theaters were seen as of little value, the Goodspeed was reborn as a venue for trying out new musical stage productions. The best of these trial runs were sent on to Broadway. The old theater is thriving in its new role. In the wake of an exterior restoration carried out in 1990, the Goodspeed—an opera house originally constructed by ship carpenters—has now been fully overhauled, inside and out.

More recent efforts to save a bit of the theatrical heritage of Times Square came to fruition with the December 1995 reopening of the oldest standing playhouse in New York's Broadway theater district. When the New Victory Theater (1900) first opened its doors as Oscar Hammerstein's Theatre Republic, its 42nd Street location was well north of the established theater district of the day. This midtown theater was built with a flight of stairs at either side of its streetfront façade, rising to meet in a broad upper landing, with its own grand entry perched above the first-level doors directly underneath. The otherwise flat-faced exterior was built using a gray Powhat-tan brick above a dark brownstone base. Inside, the high-light of the auditorium was a spoked plasterwork ceiling, with pairs of harp-playing cherubs spaced evenly around the rim.

Rival theater operator David Belasco leased the Repub-lic from Hammerstein in 1902, remodeling the interior and running it as the Belasco Theatre for the next dozen years. Again called the Republic during the years of the First World War, the theater hit another dead end under burlesque king Bill Minsky's stewardship in 1942, when Mayor Fiorello LaGuardia succeeded in banning all bur-lesque shows in the City of New York. Rechristened the Victory Theatre, Hammerstein's old showplace became a second-run movie house. Worse was to come in the 1970s, when pornographic films became its main attrac-tion. An interpretive reconstruction—part restoration, part new construction—carried out by the firm Hardy Holzman Pfeiffer Associates has since brought the place back to life as the New Victory. A headline in *The New York Times* on December 11, 1995, told the story: "An Old Jewel of 42nd Street Reopens, Seeking to Dazzle Families." Perhaps the theater has finally left its scandalous days behind for a bright new future.

Clearly no such promise exists for every nineteenth-century theatrical relic now standing empty, yet new rescue operations keep cropping up in big cities and small towns. In such efforts, even the most derelict halls should not be overlooked, given the historical memories they contain. In so many cases, fine decor is hidden only by dust, and enviable acoustics are there to be recaptured. The legacy of nineteenth-century theater design also survives in new construction, such as that of the Seiji Ozawa Concert Hall, opened in 1994 on the grounds of the Tanglewood Music Center near Lenox, Massachusetts. The hall, produced by William Rawn and Theatre Perfor-mance Associates, has a magnificently illuminated woodwork interior unlike any other modern concert hall, yet the space is strongly reminiscent of the acoustically supreme Troy Savings Bank Music Hall of 1875 in upstate New York, and of the Boston Symphony Orchestra's winter home, Symphony Hall (1900). The legacy of older halls is apparent when places like Ozawa Hall are built, but the best way to memorialize them is to preserve the buildings themselves.

The 42nd Street façade of the New Victory Theater (1900) in New York City closely approximates the original of this early Times Square venue. (Courtesy of Hardy Holzman Pfeiffer Associates)

A newcomer on the grounds of the Tanglewood Music Center, near Lenox, Massachusetts, the Seiji Ozawa Hall (1994) has a modern look combined with the style of an earlier era.

Theater Genres

T O PRESENT THE HISTORY OF AMERICA'S NINETEENTH-CENTURY performance halls in a way that does justice to such a broad range of buildings, it has been necessary to group them, somewhat loosely, into genres of theaters, based upon certain shared elements. Common elements include the reasons a specific theater was built, in terms of the community it served, as well as its intended entertainment uses. The genre of western boomtown opera houses is self-explanatory, while library theaters can be defined by their mixed-use programs. In contrast, revival halls and chautauquas were created by specific organizations to house gatherings with a moral or spiritual bent. Grand opera houses and Victorian playhouses sometimes have overlapping elements. Thus, these divisions are meant to illuminate various lines of theater development in America, as the prototypes we borrowed from Europe both branched out from as well as crossed over genres.

Two threads were clearly evident at the beginning of the nineteenth century. One can be traced to Britain, while the second is more of a homegrown variety. The English music hall was itself a hybrid form: a public house used for theatrical purposes. In these halls, there were no rows of seats on the flat main floor, and possibly none in any gallery spaces above. A serving bar might occupy the center of the hall, while the stage would be raised high and set into an opening cut into one of the walls. Such arrangements made the English music hall something of a distant cousin to the saloon theaters of the early American West, with their equally rudimentary stage layouts. More direct parentage hailed from halls along the Atlantic seaboard, whose shapes developed independently of European models as specific needs arose.

One performance space in the old center of Charleston, South Carolina, opened under the name of McCrady's Tavern (1778). Owner Edward McCrady, a soldier in the Revolutionary War, returned home to operate his tavern's "long room." A stage area, flush with the main dining hall floor, was separated only by a simple framed opening. Small-scale performances were put on to entertain honored dinner guests, such as George Washington during his state visit to the city in 1791. The tavern-theater went out of business in the mid-1800s, but was reborn as a posh restaurant a century or so later as McCrady's Long Room, where the old vestibule-stage is once again the site of the occasional performance.

The structure now known as California's First Theater (1846), in Monterey, was also opened as a drinking establishment. Local entrepreneur Jack Swan is credited with building the saloon and an attached residence wing, which later evolved into a stage.

The Lexington Opera House (1887) in Lexington, Kentucky. (LHAT)

46

Entertainments in the small saloon proved so popular that the residence wing was quickly converted into one long hall with a small stage raised slightly at the end opposite the saloon. Over time, stepped platforms were constructed at the rear end of the hall to give the back-row patrons a better view of the stage proceedings. Although not particularly stylish in design, these tavern-theaters were forerunners of the fancy playhouses of the Victorian era.

The meetinghouses of New England, parents to the town hall opera house genre, were equally plain in appearance. Given the religious foundations of these assembly buildings, they could not have been otherwise. One meetinghouse that was gradually transformed for theatrical uses still stands, the Town Hall (1789) of Washington, New Hampshire. Its exterior suggests the archetypal New England church, featuring whitewashed clapboard sides and a lantern-topped spire standing high at the northern end. The initial layout of the interior was as a single open volume with an elevated pulpit and a gallery along the other three walls. By 1820, the space had been split horizontally, and town offices were built downstairs from the new second-floor hall. Prior to 1842, when a stage was built at one end of the flat floor, both dances and religious gatherings were held upstairs.

The majority of municipal opera houses in New England and elsewhere in the country follow the layout of Washington Town Hall, in its 1820-altered format with the performance space perched above town offices. Location of these multipurpose buildings at the center of their townships is another common feature. The wooden Town Hall (1857) in Cohasset, Massachusetts, faces directly onto the common. Holley Hall (1890) in Bristol, Vermont, and Camden Opera House (1894) in Maine are similarly situated.

The tables are set this evening, but the stage is not, inside McCrady's Long Room (1778) in Charleston, South Carolina.

Many of the town hall opera houses built late in the 1800s, such as the one in Camden, had far more elaborate ornamental schemes than earlier municipal halls. Mid-century theaters tended to be more austere, like Fulton Hall (1852), which faces the main thoroughfare of Lancaster, Pennsylvania. The interior of the hall was later decorated more significantly during remodelings in 1873 and 1904, when the auditorium was known as the Fulton Opera House. The Cheney Brothers Company, a silk manufacturing concern, had a playhouse built for the company town of Manchester, Connecticut. From the outside, Cheney Hall (1867) could be mistaken for a family mansion, but its interior bears a stronger resemblance to a church. Its arched doorways, set in sidewalls at either end of the stage apron, push the space out laterally like the vestigial transept arms of a Latin-cross cathedral.

By the 1880s and 1890s, similarities to church architecture had all but disappeared from such turn-of-the-century venues as the Siasconset Casino (1900), an island playhouse in Massachusetts. Although such casinos sported flat floors and were built primarily of wood, these venues were otherwise light years removed from the

Jack Swan's original tavern was expanded into a showplace, now known as California's First Theater (1846), in Monterey.

Above: Washington Town Hall (1789) sits atop a rise on the old common of this New Hampshire town named for our first president.

Right: Cheney Hall (1867) was built to entertain factory workers and their families in Manchester, Connecticut.

Above: The Fulton Opera House (1852) in Lancaster, Pennsylvania, looked somewhat more austere in its early days before the addition of its electric marquee. (Fulton Opera House Foundation/LHAT)

Overleaf: The auditorium of the Pabst Theater (1895) in Milwaukee blends Old World traditions with the innovations of nineteenth-century theater design in America. (LHAT)

rudimentary meetinghouses and plain-jane town halls. The casino designs were proof of a comfortably established population, in contrast to the founding settlers who had to work to secure a foothold in the fledgling United States. Even recent immigrants found prosperity in late nineteenth-century America, and often built theaters as markers of their success. Such was the case in Milwaukee, where former steamboat captain Frederick Pabst used the profits from his brewing empire to fund construction of the triple-tiered Pabst Theater (1895). The strongest influence on its architect, Otto Strack, was not his familiarity with European concert halls, but rather the design of Adler & Sullivan's Auditorium Theater, opened six years earlier in nearby Chicago. Like Milwaukee's founding German immigrants, America's theaters were descended from foreign stock, but took firm root in their new country. The architectural seeds first planted in the young American garden had been well tended. By the end of the century, America's native varieties of theaters and concert halls came into bloom.

A Revue of Nineteenth-Century American

THEATERS

There are two contrasting faces to the combined city hall–theater Thalian Hall (1858) in Wilmington, North Carolina. The current color scheme and interior configuration date back to a remodeling carried out in 1909.

Opposite: Trumpeting cherubs crown the opera boxes inside the Portsmouth Music Hall (1878) in New Hampshire.

Above: The City Hall Opera House (1893) in Sumter, South Carolina, was revamped in 1936, for its new use as a movie house.

Above: The City Theater (1896) in Biddeford, Maine, is a relative study in simplicity compared to the Earlville Opera House (1892) in upstate New York, with its fancy woodwork proscenium arch and pressed-tin ceiling.

Opposite: The Thomaston Opera House (1884) in Connecticut is a full-sized theater wrapped up inside the brick-and-stone mass of the Thomaston City Hall Building.

Opposite: Thin posts mark the curve of a horseshoe balcony inside the What Cheer Opera House (1893) in Iowa.

Above: The grand lobby of the Pabst Theater (1895) in Milwaukee, Wisconsin, is lined with marble,

while Apollo presides within the upper reaches of the main auditorium above the proscenium arch.

Overleaf: Silver magnate Jerome B. Wheeler constructed the Wheeler Opera House (1889) in Aspen, Colorado.

After decades as a movie house, the Eureka Opera House (1880) in Nevada used gold bullion tax dollars to renovate the building as a theater and conference center. (Courtesy of Eureka Opera House)

Opposite: Bullet holes
pockmark the surface of the
Bird Cage Theatre (1881) in the
once–Wild West boomtown
of Tombstone, Arizona.

Above: The main attraction
at the Central City Opera
House (1878) in Colorado
really is opera, performed
throughout the Rocky Mountain summers. (Courtesy of
Central City Opera House)

Overleaf: Mechanics Hall (1857)
in Worcester, Massachusetts,
offers a spectacular pipe organ.

The Grand Opera House (1890)
in Meridian, Mississippi, is
still functioning but in need
of some major repairs.

Above and opposite:
The Mabel Tainter Memorial
Theater (1890) in
Menomonie, Wisconsin,

was erected in memory of
the third child of Wisconsin
lumber baron Andrew Tainter
and his second wife, Bertha.

The town hall offices came with a fancy port cochere attached as part of the library-theater ensemble of Cumston Hall (1900) in Monmouth, Maine. Cherubs play in the imitation moonlight of the lantern fresco above the main floor seats.

Overleaf: The Haskell Opera House (1904) divides itself between Derby Line, Vermont, and Rock Island, Quebec.

Opposite: Symphony
Hall (1899) in Allentown,
Pennsylvania, was in
business as a farmer's market
before it was refashioned
by theater specialists
J. B. McElfatrick & Sons.

Above: The old lobby space
of the Folly Theater (1900)
in Missouri was updated and
the exterior repaired, thanks
to the generous support
shown by local patrons of
the arts in Kansas City.

Above: The compositional elegance of the uniquely subterranean Steinert Hall (1896) still shines through despite decades of non-theatrical uses.

Opposite: Painted plasterwork enlivens the auditorium of Boston's Colonial Theatre (1900).

The eminently Victorian decor is just one of the treats of the Academy of Music (1891) in Northampton, Massachusetts.

Above: The Goodspeed Opera House (1877) in East Haddam, Connecticut, sports a fanciful treble clef on the side of the stage.

Opposite: Patrons of the Grand Opera House (1871) in Wilmington, Delaware, sit beneath the star-studded "sky" of its central oculus.

Above: A stylish throwback to the opera houses of Europe, the Philadelphia Academy of Music (1857) possesses an unflagging vitality befitting the chief representative of the city's long and storied theatrical history.

Opposite: The Grand 1894 Opera House of Galveston, Texas, is among American theatre's finest architectural creations.

Opposite: The great volume
of the Chicago Auditorium
Theater (1889) rises to include
a pair of galleries above
the main balcony seating.

Above: The Cincinnati Music
Hall (1878) is a grand-scaled
venue designed by the firm
of Hannaford & Proctor.
(Phil Groshong/Courtesty of
Cincinnati Music Hall)

Eastern Town Hall Opera Houses

Opposite: The Stockbridge
Town Hall (1893) in Michigan
sits amidst the trees of the
town square.

Below: Stick Style patterning
enlivens the exterior of the
Brimfield Town Hall (1879)
in Massachusetts.

THE OBVIOUS LINKS BETWEEN MUNICIPAL GOVERNMENT OFFICES
and public meeting spaces brought a multitude of town hall opera
houses into being. In such combination venues, the assembly hall could
be attached to the city hall in any number of ways, but the typical
arrangement was to put the performance space on the upper floor,
above the town offices. (Clearly, weekday matinees were not common
in those days.) Given their upper-story locations, these opera houses generally had
flat floors, with wooden surfaces, whose seats were not built in, to allow for maximum
versatility. If additional seating was required, it usually took the form of either a three-
sided gallery or a shelf balcony, with a horseshoe-shape the preferred design for fancier
halls. The simple configurations of these flat-floored opera houses could easily accommodate a town meeting one day and a touring band show the next, with a dress ball
in the evening between.

For the most part, town hall opera houses tended to be modest in decor, often as
simple as their direct ancestors, the New England meetinghouses. Both types were
bare by design, but the town halls were so for reasons of public economy rather than
for spiritual concerns. The Hardwick Town House (1850) in Vermont even has the look
of a church, particularly with its whitewashed clapboard exterior and its rows of
pewlike seats. Elsewhere in the state, the Town Hall (1860) in South Londonderry
features a tall steeple at its front, but its interior hall, covered by elaborate woodwork

design is less church-like. Massachusetts theaters of this
type include Brimfield Town Hall (1879) and Old Town
Hall (1881) in Brewster. The Brimfield landmark might still
be mistaken for a meetinghouse, despite its fanciful Stick
Style exterior. In contrast, Brewster Town Hall, with its
stylish port cochere, would more likely be mistaken for
a Cape Cod estate than a religious assembly hall.

Resurgent industrial growth in New England, following
the end of the Civil War in 1865, eventually led to town
hall designs that were, on the whole, much more elaborate than the antebellum variety. Many quiet wooded
towns became prosperous manufacturing centers, enabling
them to build grand city halls, often including full-scale
theaters under the same tall roof. Thomaston, Connecticut, originally known as Thomas Town, is home to the
factory that manufactured Seth Thomas clocks. An opulent
525-seat theater was included in the plan when an
immense new Town Hall (1884), clad in brick and stone,
was built a short distance upriver from the clockworks.

The City Theater (1896) in the elaborately massed City Hall of Biddeford, Maine, is an even larger example of this theater genre with fifty more seats than its Connecticut cousin. It is important to note that despite the multipurpose use of these two town halls, both building exteriors are not only majestic but also unified in appearance.

The powerful brick exterior of Town Hall in Lancaster, New York, has a Romanesque Revival look, thanks to architect George J. Metzger. The Lancaster Opera House (1897) opened on the building's third and fourth floors, but not until three years after the town offices had been completed downstairs. The theater has a raked stage, inclined at a ratio of one-half inch per foot from front to back. The proscenium is framed by matching pairs of wooden columns, each wrapped in twisting foliage, also carved in wood. An equally impressive town hall in New York encloses the Fredonia Opera House (1891). Even the rear wall of this red-brick building is attractive, its rounded corners matching the curves of circular stairwells tucked inside either end of the theater stagehouse.

Upstairs town hall opera houses, most numerous in the New England states, occasionally sprouted up elsewhere in the country. Among the survivors in the South is the Pocahontas (Virginia) Opera House (1895), built above the town's municipal courts and its adjacent holding cells. The lower level of the Newberry (South Carolina) Opera House (1882) once included the central fire station, in addition to the town jail and municipal offices. City officials initiated renovation plans for the building in 1995, in order to repair the stonework entry arch and reinstate a wraparound gallery inside the auditorium.

Sumter, South Carolina, lost its original Town Hall Opera House (1872) to a fire that started in one of the dressing rooms in 1892. The new Opera House that opened in City Hall the following year cost townspeople $35,000, a princely sum in those days, but nevertheless a bargain. Architect J. C. Turner of Augusta, Georgia, centered his design for the building on a great four-sided clock tower, faced with buff-colored Cumberland stone and massed in the Renaissance Revival style made popular in that period by Boston architect Henry Hobson Richardson. Those who enter the main-level auditorium today are in for a shock, however, because the space was transformed into an Art Moderne-style movie theater in 1936. In those Depression days, admission prices were still fairly cheap in Sumter: tickets were ten cents for children and thirty-five cents for grown-ups.

Among the upstairs town hall opera houses built in the Great Lakes region, one standout is the Stockbridge Town Hall (1893) in Michigan, situated at the center of the tree-covered town square. Its architect was Elijah E. Myers, who also designed the state's Capitol Building in East Lansing. Downstairs from the Town Hall, a gracefully proportioned auditorium with attractive timber trusswork, are the former town offices (now used as the town's firefighter and rescue squad base).

It is difficult to determine the exact number of town hall opera houses constructed

Above: Thomaston Opera House (1884) occupies the upper half of this Connecticut town hall building.

Opposite: City Hall in Biddeford, Maine, conceals the City Theater (1896) within its high-spired exterior.

The upstairs hall of the Saco City Hall in Saco, Maine, acquired renewed dignity following renovation work carried out in 1994. The clock tower was added to the building in 1888.

in this country. Beyond the fifty or so still fit for public meetings and theatrical performances, many other halls survive but are empty or used minimally. The former upstairs opera hall in Smyrna, Delaware, now serves as storage space for the town library, which moved into the lower floor when the city offices transferred to a new building nearby. The city council chambers of Franklin, New Hampshire, occupy the first-floor space that once held the main-floor seating of the theater formerly known as Soldier's Memorial Hall, now the Franklin Opera House (1892). The old balcony area is sealed off, its tiered levels given over for general storage. The possible reconversion of this city hall building, credited to architect H. H. Richardson, to its theatrical origins was under study in 1995.

In these halls that sit vacant or misused, a critical piece of a town's past waits to be recaptured. Much of a community's public life took place inside these buildings: government affairs, social events, school graduations, and, perhaps, the first movie screenings. Unfortunately, during the nineteenth century, some towns took these buildings for granted as newer theaters were built, although this attitude did not go unnoticed by all. The somber Hardwick Town House in Vermont was not accorded full respect, much to the dismay of at least one town resident. One Mr. Sawyer, writing in 1899, chastised his neighbors: "The fact that we have the finest opera house of any town anywhere our size is something to be proud of. But if terbacker [sic] juice shows which way the men squirt, we shall soon have to connect the floor with the sewer, or wear rubber boots and life preservers when we get there. Someone has intimated that if patrons of the place must chew, spittoons be delivered with all tickets sold, or that ushers, armed with tubs on long poles, pass with slow-moving regularity about the house, giving all who wish a chance to expectorate." There is no record that any of Mr. Sawyer's facetious remedies were ever adopted. Still, the Town House survives, in near-spotless condition, a century later.

Opposite: The main hall of the Pocahontas Opera House (1895) in Virginia sits atop the former town courtroom.

Above: Work in 1995 restored the stonework entry arch of South Carolina's Newberry Opera House (1882), with the upstairs auditorium next in line for renovations.

The rusticated stonework of City Hall (1893) dominates the center of Sumter, South Carolina. Its Opera House became a movie house in 1936.

Chester Meetinghouse

This whitewashed clapboard structure first opened its doors as the Second Congregational Meetinghouse of the Fourth Parish of Saybrook (a town near what is now Chester). According to a plaque outside the Meetinghouse, the building was acquired by the Town of Chester in 1847, at a price of $1,300, after the residing congregation built a new church in another part of the area. The Meetinghouse was much smaller at that time; the stage and balcony were not constructed until 1876. The following spring, Chester townspeople voted that "the Hall be opened to citizens of the town for any purpose at the direction of the Selectmen." In the years since, the purposes have been diverse: town meetings alternated with theatre performances, dances, recitals, and graduations. By 1960, however, the Meetinghouse was deemed obsolete, when the town voted to include a public auditorium as part of its new elementary school. Thus, the Meetinghouse stood empty for a decade.

A domestic-scaled exterior conceals the main hall of the Chester Meetinghouse. The theater was in the throes of renovation in 1995.

Then the Chester Historical Society decided to use the hall for its gatherings. By the fall of 1972, the building had been added to the National Register of Historic Places, and a restoration committee began a fund drive for the purpose of renovating the interior. On Memorial Day 1973, a community reception was held to celebrate the reopening of the Meetinghouse. A second refurbishment of the auditorium was completed in 1995.

Through all the changes in use and condition, the Meetinghouse has remained modest in size. The auditorium is among the smallest public halls in the country, measuring 44 feet across and just 30 feet from front to back. Nevertheless, the main floor, together with the tightly curving balcony, can seat as many as 215 people. Decked out with polished mahogany woodwork, its walls now painted a bright pink, the space seems hardly larger and is equally as charming as the town bandstand, directly across the park onto which the Meetinghouse faces. The two structures share dollhouse construction, even as they retain their larger roles in the life of this town and its inhabitants.

Provincetown Town Hall

PROVINCETOWN, MASSACHUSETTS, 1886

In its heyday, the Town Hall at the center of Provincetown was the setting of some notorious goings-on. During the years between the world wars, crowds comprising an assortment of famous and lesser-known local and summer residents eagerly anticipated the annual Artists and Beachcombers Balls. These were typically masquerade balls and a little on the wild side. One year the prize for best costume was a guernsey bull calf. Other animals that made an appearance in the third-floor auditorium included those "playing" in the occasional donkey basketball tournaments. By comparison, today within the restrained decor of the theater, a more typical program of concerts and plays is presented.

The Town Hall building, which includes the town offices, the police station, and the jail, was constructed under the guidance of architect John A. Fox of Boston. The previous town hall, lost to fire in 1877, was located on Monument Hill (known earlier as High Pole Hill). After years with no main public building, the town decided to build a new hall nearer to its central district. Reverend Henry Ryder donated the land, which included an apple orchard at its northern end. The new Town Hall, dedicated August 25, 1886, cost $50,400 to build, including the appointments for the 1,000-seat auditorium.

The whitewashed wooden building is capped by a great clock tower, the bequest of a local resident. Original interior amenities included steam heat and gas lighting. And despite the then-remote location of Provincetown on the extreme tip of Cape Cod, according to management records, a sufficient local workforce was available, enabling operators of the theater to obtain full sets of scenery during the Depression era for about $100. No account books survive that show the costs of the beachcomber balls or the donkey basketball games, but you have to imagine they were worth every penny.

Opposite: A bronze soldier commemorating townsmen who fought in World War I stands sentry by the Provincetown Town Hall.

Below: A vintage postcard shows the view west from Town Hall, here at the tip of Cape Cod. (*The Provincetown Advocate*)

Published for The Provincetown Advocate.

Town Hall and R. R. Wharf from Town Hill, Provincetown, Mass.

Opposite: This sedate
view of the Provincetown
auditorium belies its past

as site to the sometimes
rowdy Beachcombers Balls in
the early part of this century.

Above: The Town Hall building
includes town offices, the
police station, and the jail.

Claremont Opera House

The great mass that is the Claremont City Hall and Opera House was constructed with nearly one million Lebanon bricks, hauled across the state and set on a foundation of local Green Mountain stone. The cladding of the street-level exterior, as well as the ornamental flourishes of the upper stories and the clock tower, were composed of brownstone taken from the Connecticut River near Springfield, Massachusetts. Architect Charles A. Rich, in practice in New York City after graduating from nearby Dartmouth College, designed the building in the Italian Renaissance Revival style popular at the time.

Claremont prospered greatly in the late nineteenth century, thanks to the abundant water power available from the nearby Sugar River. The City Hall and Opera House were begun in 1896 to take the place of an earlier meetinghouse that the town had outgrown. Proud of its growing regional prominence, town leaders asked architect Rich to include

Above: The Claremont Opera House has an especially light touch to its plasterwork decor. (David S. Putnam/LHAT)

Opposite: The Claremont City Hall is composed of brick and stone, all hauled to town from different sites around New England.

the State Seal of New Hampshire twice in the overall design of the building. It is set into a stonework cartouche on the street face of the clock tower and in a frescoed medallion above the proscenium arch.

While the city offices face west, onto the town's commercial heart around Tremont Square, the second-floor opera house is contained within the portion of the building facing the old town commons, now called Broad Street Park. A sense of the outdoors is worked into the color scheme of the Opera House interior. The dominant beige is accented in forest green and dark brown. The decorative artistry of the interior is of such a high order that not even the iron tie-rods spanning the auditorium ceiling detract from the elegance. The fresco work was executed by a crew of five employees from the Boston firm Schupbach & Zeller. Above the main-floor seating, the balcony design, surrounded by a wooden grille, moves in an easy curve and counter-curves. The ceiling has a grillwork dome, measuring 10 feet in diameter and lit by forty-eight incandescent bulbs, each set in a fixture with a gilded-laurel motif. The crowning feature of the interior design is the gilt plaster mask of Thespis, centered above the proscenium arch and flanked by trumpeting cherubs executed in plaster.

In its early years, the Opera House also served as an assembly hall. Before the Depression, a local druggist, Harry Eaton, moonlighted as its manager, and during his long tenure, he introduced Claremont residents to Saturday matinees and such major touring shows as *John Philip Sousa's Band of Fifty*. The Opera House was closed in 1963, but was given a second life in 1977 when it reopened with the help of a federal preservation grant, supplemented by local conservation monies.

Thalian Hall

WILMINGTON, NORTH CAROLINA, 1858

This thriving showplace, opened as the Wilmington Theatre, maintains one of the busiest schedules in the country. The Thalian Hall of today mixes top touring shows with local events that have always been a trademark of this theater. Aside from the short period in 1865 when an attack by federal troops on nearby Fort Fisher caused the hall to close, the theater has enjoyed steady business since it opened October 12, 1858. The name Thalian Hall dates to 1932, the year the local Thalian Association assumed full-time residency. (Prior to that time, the hall had been available for general lease.) Attached to the Wilmington City Hall, the theater has been home to its share of local recitals, school graduations, and, at some time in the 1880s, rollerskating. The earliest recorded productions were staged here in 1875 by the Thalian Dramatic Combination Company. Guest lecturers in the late 1800s included Booker T. Washington and Frederick Douglass. Thomas Edison scheduled a week in 1897 at the Thalian to display his new Projectoscope. A granite marker, near where City Hall abuts the Thalian, commemorates an address given in Wilmington by President Taft in 1909.

The theater wing, together with City Hall, are the work of John Montague Trimble of New York. Since the razing in 1959 of the Buffalo Academy of Music in Trimble's home state, Thalian Hall stands as the only surviving work by this architect. The green, gold, and red color scheme of the auditorium is not original. This palette, selected in 1909, overlays plasterwork balcony fronts and cast-iron columns, which were part of the original design. The exterior of the theater, now white, was built of bricks covered by a layer of stucco, which initially was scored and painted to suggest a reddish brownstone. The original entrance to the hall is no longer in use. Access now is gained primarily through a new entry block that was added as part of the Master Plan of 1983, adopted and implemented over the following seven years.

A comfortable blend of old and new, Thalian Hall retains a number of features that might have been lost during alterations. In addition to the cannonball-operated thunder run, the backstage still has an old windlass used for hauling scenery. And a painted stage curtain that was taken down from the house front now hangs in a place of honor on one wall of the lobby. In the upper gallery, backless benches are topped by cushions stuffed with corn husks, reminders of the era when segregated seating areas were common in America. Consequently, Thalian Hall is a showplace that reveals more of our history than theatrical and architectural features.

Opposite: The auditorium decor inside Thalian Hall shows a sense of neo-Palladian classicism. (Thalian Hall Archives Collection)

Below: Vintage stage drapery has been hung on permanent display in the lobby.

Theatrical Venues in the Midwest

THEATER BUILDERS IN THE MIDWESTERN STATES TENDED NOT to follow the town hall model popular in New England. They preferred to mix business and recreation architecturally, by building performance spaces set at the cores of commercial office blocks or above a row of shops. The Genoa Opera House (1885) in Ohio is a rare exception, more akin to eastern halls, with its auditorium above the town council chambers. More typical of theaters in Ohio is the Victoria Theatre (1866), first known as the Turner Opera House, in Dayton. Although converted in the 1920s into a movie house, this venue still has the look of a nineteenth-century mercantile block. Other notable halls in Ohio include the Majestic Theatre (1853), in Chillicothe, and the Sorg Opera House (1891), in Middletown. The Majestic assumed its current role as a play-house only after serving as a Masonic temple, a vaudeville house, and a morgue for soldiers who died in training for World War I. The Sorg Opera House has an impressive stonework entry arch at the base of a five-story office block. Patrons must still traverse a long, narrow lobby to reach the auditorium, which is located at the back of the office building, but the decor is worth the walk.

The builders of the Southern Theatre (1896) in Columbus, Ohio, borrowed heavily from Adler & Sullivan's design for the Auditorium Theater (1889) in Chicago. Chief designer Menno S. Detweiler had worked in Chicago on the 1893 World's Columbian Exposition. In Columbus, he gave the Southern's auditorium a set of illuminated arches more fully rounded than those in Chicago's landmark theater by Adler & Sullivan. Detweiler's client in Columbus, the Great Southern Fireproof Hotel Company, required that the Southern be incorporated into a huge block fronted by a new grand hotel. Although the theater's entry doors are on the side of the building, they are easy to find, thanks to a monumental entry arch carved in stone. The Southern originally seated 1,723 patrons on three levels, plus the staggered opera boxes along the side walls. Scheduled renovation of the theater, along with the encasing hotel, will reduce the capacity of the Southern to approximately 900 seats.

The Columbian Theatre (1895) in Wamego, Kansas, also has ties to Chicago and the 1893 exposition. Known initially as the Rogers Music Hall, the venue opened with a Grand Ball on New Year's Eve in 1895. Local businessman J. C. Rogers built the theater on the second floor above his mercantile operation. Not only had Rogers attended the Chicago fair, but he also managed to salvage six from a set of eight painted murals that had decorated the walls of the U.S. Treasury Department's Government Pavilion. The eight allegorical scenes, from the hand of artist Emil Philipson, were meant to depict

The Valparaiso Memorial Opera House (1893) is a popular venue in this Indiana college town.

the leading economic forces of late nineteenth-century America by showing farmlands and steel mills operated by hardworking cherubs. The other two scenes reputedly were purchased by another buyer to beautify the lobby of a new office block in Kansas City, Missouri. Rogers brought the other six to Wamego, where they were incorporated in the design of his new theater.

Among the earliest freestanding theaters west of the Mississippi was Thespian Hall (1857) in Boonville, Missouri. The town's Thespian Society, formed in 1838, raised funds by giving benefit performances over three years to build this imposing Greek Revival building. The theater group did not outlast the Civil War, however, and ownership of the hall passed to the Turn Verein, a local choral and gymnastic society formed by German immigrants. The theater basement served as an armory during the war, and afterwards was transformed into a roller rink. The entire interior of the theater was remodeled in 1901 by architect J. L. Howard of St. Louis into the configuration that survives to this day.

At least two grand-scale city hall opera houses survive in Illinois: the Sandwich Opera House (1878) and the Woodstock Opera House (1890). Smith Hoag, the architect for the Woodstock hall, situated the building right on the town square. Its auditorium eventually served as a proving ground for the young Orson Welles, who was enrolled in 1934 as a student at the nearby Todd School for Boys. A permanent summer stock company took up residence at the Woodstock Opera House in 1947.

A bell tower caps the Town Hall (1885) in Genoa, Ohio.

Such broad diversity of style and configuration among midwestern venues is due only in part to the absence of a strong model comparable to the meetinghouses of New England. Prior to the late-century pairing of Adler & Sullivan, there were few architects in the region with much experience designing theaters, aside from the Ohio firm of Hannaford & Proctor. (In addition to working with Proctor on the Cincinnati Music Hall of 1878, Samuel Hannaford designed the Sorg Opera House in Middletown.) With no single dominant architectural force like H. H. Richardson in the East, midwestern designers followed their own minds, producing some unique creations (the Mabel Tainter Memorial of 1890, a library theater in Menomonie, Wisconsin, foremost among them). Different was not always better, but the region does not lack its share of major showplaces.

Above: The handsome exterior of Dayton's Victoria Theatre has been slightly modified from its original 1866 appearance. (Victoria Theatre Association/LHAT)

Left: A rehearsal onstage at the Majestic Theatre (1853) in Chillicothe, Ohio.

The auditorium of the Sorg
Opera House in Middletown,
Ohio, is located behind this
1891 vintage office block. (LHAT)

The Southern Theatre in
Columbus, Ohio, as it appeared
for its opening in 1896.
(Columbus Association
for the Performing Arts/LHAT)

The Columbian Theatre (1895), showplace of Wamego, Kansas, is pictured in a 1927 view. (Courtesy of Marc Stratton)

Above: Tall brick columns dominate the front of Thespian Hall (1857) in Boonville, Missouri.

Opposite: Stone trim adds stateliness to the exterior of the Woodstock City Hall (1890) in Illinois. (LHAT)

Calumet Theater

At the turn of the century, this town, made rich by nearby copper mines, was still known as Red Jacket. The Calumet Theater and new town offices replaced the old Red Jacket Opera House of 1887, which likewise had shared a roof with the old town hall. Opening night ticket prices for the new theater, on March 20, 1900, started at one dollar. A seat in one of the small opera boxes at either end of the stage cost a princely $25.00. And to ensure that all the Upper Peninsula patrons could make the show on time, extra trains were put into service for this one special evening. Even before they entered the theater, patrons were treated to the sight of a brilliant electric sign. Inside, they witnessed the spectacle of a reported 1,441 incandescent lights, 275 of which were used just to outline the proscenium arch. After the lights were dimmed for the performance, patrons were startled by the sight of a live horse onstage during the pivotal holdup scene of the play. Little wonder the newspapers called the opening "the greatest social event known in Copperdom's Metropolis."

Above: The off-street view of the Calumet Theater reveals a slightly less refined side of the building.

Opposite: Good views are to be had by all inside the Calumet Theater.

The conjoined theater and city hall were designed by architect Charles K. Shand of Detroit, and built at a cost just under $60,000. A four-sided clock tower anchors the building, with its fanciful Renaissance Revival brick design set above a streetfront port cochere constructed of rusticated stonework. Safety concerns led the Red Jacket Village Council to add a fire escape to one side of the building in 1901, following an opening year marked frequently by sold-out performances.

Prosperity did not last long, however. Despite the claims of one councilman that Red Jacket wasn't just "a Klondike boomtown," the area's mineral wealth was depleted shortly after the theater was completed. Among the few reminders of Calumet's glorious past, while still the Village of Red Jacket, is the hundred-bulb copper chandelier, which still shines in the theater auditorium. The lights come in handy for the occasional touring show, and, since 1972, summer stock productions, which were initiated by Michigan State University. Calumet itself has undergone something of a renaissance over the years, its boomtown architectural heritage proving a tourist draw. All the attention can only help the Calumet Theater keep its many lights ablaze.

What Cheer Opera House

The origin of the name for both this quiet town and its 600-seat theater is a matter of some uncertainty among local residents. "What Cheer!" is apparently a salutation that originated in England or Wales, and became popular among the miners who settled this town in the historic heart of the coal-mining district in Iowa. The original settlement was known as Petersburgh, but when a post office was built in 1879, the name somehow became What Cheer.

Architect J. J. Gordineer designed the opera house in 1893 for the local chapter of Masons, who opened the hall the following February with a gala ball in the third-floor meeting room. The first performance in the main-floor theater followed three weeks later. Special trains brought people in from the surrounding towns of Belle Plaine, South English, and Montezuma, to share in the official opening of the What Cheer Opera House.

The theater has since found a place in the *Guiness Book of World Records*, thanks to a special door built along one exterior wall of the stagehouse for scenery handling. The door is 12 feet 2 inches high, but measures only 1 foot 7 inches wide, making it, in terms of relative proportions, the narrowest door in the world.

Celebrations of the town's centennial in 1965 brought renewed interest in the Opera House, which had been vacant for years. A not-for-profit corporation was formed to raise funds for the renovation of the hall, and the What Cheer Opera House was swinging again by April 1966, to the music of Guy Lombardo and his Royal Canadians. Its doors, broad and narrow, have been open ever since.

The Opera House is on the main floor beneath the old Masonic meeting rooms.

Grand Opera House

The Grand Opera House of Oshkosh was a product of civic philanthropy, first conceived as a gift to the town by the Oshkosh Men's Association in January 1882. This group directed architect William Waters and artist J. F. Waldo to design the theater along conventional Old World lines. Thus, the fussily ornate interior scheme is more in keeping with the tastes of the late Victorian period. The auditorium is roughly a cubic volume. A pair of boxes, stacked on either side of the stage, break into the cube, and a graceful balustraded balcony curves around the back of the house to connect the two upper boxes. Tall side walls, their tops decorated with stylized floral stencilwork, merge overhead to form the edges of a cove ceiling.

The original lighting system for the Grand Opera House was provided by two hundred gas jets, including the eighty-two incorporated into the central "sun-burner" chandelier. The electric lights introduced two years after the opera house opened were subtly integrated into the decorative scheme. The chief appeal of the exterior of the building derives from the architect's choice of cladding material, the pinkish Cream City bricks for which Milwaukee is famous.

Since its opening night production of *The Bohemian Girl*, until its conversion to a full-time movie house in the 1940s, the theater has fulfilled its founders' dreams by serving as the central showplace for Oshkosh. A subsequent decline in fortune, when X-rated features became the standard bill of fare, was halted in 1965 with the formation of the Grand Opera House Committee, Inc. The group raised funds for a lengthy process of renovation work, whose happy result was a grand reopening in 1986.

Opposite: This view of the Oshkosh Grand Opera House may date to its opening season. (Courtesy of Oshkosh Grand Opera House)

Right: The Grand Opera House sits in easy repose near the center of Oshkosh.

Pella Opera House

PELLA, IOWA, 1900

Located at the center of this Tulip Belt town, the Pella Opera Block is ideally positioned to preside over the hoopla of the annual Tulip Time Festival. Occupying the two upper floors in a tall brick commercial block, the Opera House was opened November 16, 1900, as a public hall sponsored by town businesspeople, then sold to a private owner less than two years later. Stable management proved elusive, however, and the property changed hands nineteen more times prior to the start of World War I. By the end of the war, the Opera House had become a movie house.

Today, little remains of the original interior decor, as designed by architect Stanley de Gooyer. Long gone are the original 950 "noiseless ball-bearing opera seats." A light green and gold color scheme was applied to the walls and pressed-tin ceiling of the auditorium during renovation work carried out in the late 1980s, and a new wing and additional space were added to the backstage. At that time, a bit of the Opera House's past was rediscovered, when the original fire curtain was found rolled up in the Opera Block attic.

The street façade of this downtown block still looks as good as new, with ornate stained-glass windows set into the first-floor transoms and filling a row of circular portholes just above the second story. Whatever indignities the building may have suffered during years as a roller rink, a market, and a hardware store are forgotten since the reborn Pella Opera House Block has regained its role as grand marshal of Franklin Street, at Tulip Time or any time.

Opposite: The 1900 Opera Block holds sway above Franklin Street in Pella, Iowa. (Courtesy of Pella Opera House)

Right: Painted stencils and pressed-tin decorate the upper realm of the Pella Opera House. (Courtesy of Pella Opera House)

Pabst Theater

On January 15, 1895, Milwaukee's venerable Stadt Theatre (opened as the Nunnemacher Grand Opera House in 1871) was felled by a devastating fire. The efforts of four local fire companies could not forestall complete destruction of the building. It was inconceivable to residents of this city that they go for long without a home for their German-language theater company and its symphony orchestra, so before the end of 1895, Captain Frederick Pabst and his son Gustave put up a new theater building on the site of the Stadt. Pabst had emigrated to the United States from Germany with his parents at age twelve. In his youth, he trained aboard steamboats on Lake Michigan. He had risen to the rank of captain before his move to Milwaukee and his marriage in 1862 to Marie Best, the daughter of a prominent Milwaukee brewer.

The exterior of the Pabst Theater (1895) reflects the richness within.

The design for the Pabst Theater was created by Otto Strack, a German-born architect, who had studied in Berlin and Vienna before arriving in the American Midwest in 1888 and taking the post of supervising architect for the Pabst Brewing Company. By the time Strack arrived in the city, the three-hundred-barrel-a-year brewery Pabst had inherited from his father-in-law had grown to be the world's largest beer producer, with an annual production of two million barrels.

Almost immediately after the Stadt's destruction, Otto Strack and Gustave Pabst took a tour of nearby opera houses, paying particular attention to Chicago's Auditorium Theater. Strack's admiration for this earlier masterpiece is most apparent in his handling of technical matters at the Pabst. Strack included not only a full range of hydraulic stage machinery in his design, but also installed the first all-electric stage lighting system in the country.

As much as any other architect of his day, Strack had the capability to blend technology and artistry. This talent can be seen in the way that the sweeping balcony and gallery railings act as stiffeners in the Pabst's overall structural design. The interior decor is gloriously sumptuous, a reflection of Strack's education in European cities where he came in close contact with masterpieces of baroque architecture.

Remarkably, ornate as it is, the Pabst Theater was completed in just a few months, opening November 9, 1895, with the German Stock Company production of *Zwei Wappen*, a comedy direct from Berlin. The theater was an immediate success; the *Milwaukee Journal* reported that the Pabst had taken "the front place of the front rank of American theaters."

The original triple-tiered auditorium designed by Strack had seating for 1,820 patrons, counting the chairs in the fourteen opera boxes. Seating was reduced to 1,640, and the boxes were removed, during a remodeling carried out in 1928 by Dick & Bauer, which had just completed the city's Oriental Theater. The present chandelier was installed at that time, and the predominant color shifted from red to green. Left undisturbed during the changes were the metal grillwork seatbacks of the upper gallery, whose headrests read PABST. Appropriately, they remain in place to this day.

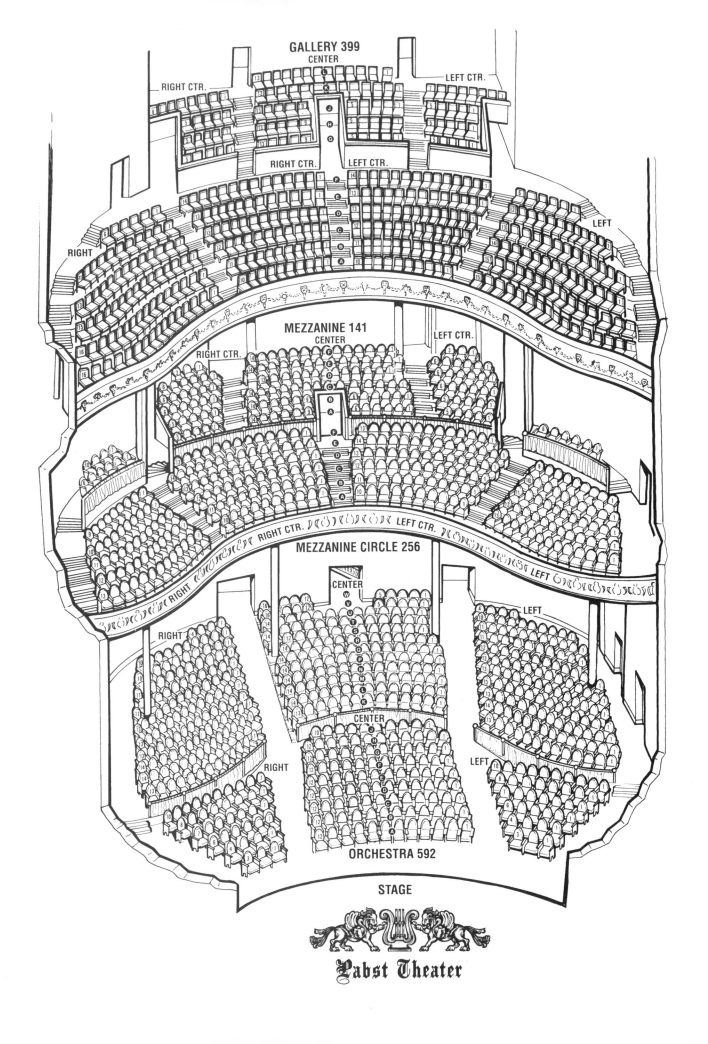

GALLERY 399

ORCHESTRA 592

STAGE

Pabst Theater

The Pabst is noted for its impressive detail and excellent acoustics. The dramatic height of the hall is graphically represented in the theater's seating chart. (Hans Keerl/LHAT)

Western Boomtown Opera Houses

THE CALIFORNIA GOLD RUSH OF 1849 WAS JUST THE BEGINNING. When the Comstock Lode strike along the Nevada border was followed by more silver strikes along the length of the Rockies, new towns sprang up almost magically and disappeared just as quickly when the mines ran dry. But between boom and bust, some semblance of conventional community life was carried on. Given enough time, theaters—some just glorified saloons—were built. In more fortunate towns, where the earth's riches were greater, the theaters were often substantial, some even opulent.

Because of the makeshift character of boomtowns, many would-be theater operators simply tacked performance spaces onto commercial buildings already in place. After fire destroyed much of the gold rush town of Columbia, California, in 1857, Owen Fallon bought a surviving hotel. Over the next six years, he attached a dance hall and a bar to the hotel. Only after his son James added a proper stage more than two decades later did his father's investment pan out as the Fallon Hotel and Theatre (1886). When the town went bust just before the turn of the century, the theater was left vacant. In 1945, the University of the Pacific brought renewed life to the Fallon, adopting the venue as its home for summer stock productions. The Columbia Actors Rep has since become the theater's resident company.

Ten years after the Great Fire of 1875 in Virginia City, Nevada, the town benefited from the tenacity of theater entrepreneur John Piper. No stranger to conflagrations, Piper saw fire destroy two earlier theaters, before he built his finest showplace, Piper's Opera House (1885). Like his previous halls, the new Opera House was designed to entertain the mine owners and prospectors living off the riches of the nearby Comstock Lode. One memorable event in the history of this venue was a production of *Hamlet* starring the famous nineteenth-century actor Edwin Booth. To enact the scene where Hamlet leaps into Ophelia's open grave, Booth jumped through a hole cut through the stage floor and landed on the bedrock underneath the theater. Piper's now hosts a few select shows every summer, since the town has come back to life as a tourist center following the closing of the mines in 1950.

The discovery of silver, lead, and zinc near Pioche, Nevada, in 1865 brought this boomtown into full-blown prosperity. A period of lawless chaos followed the strikes, prompting the town to build its Million Dollar Courthouse in 1872. Brown's Hall opened a year later in 1873 as a setting for local dances, political rallies, and dramatic

The old wooden front of the 1888 South San Francisco Opera House, later known as the Bayview, has been freshly painted to face its second century.

presentations. Renamed Thompson's Opera House in 1892, for many years, the hall hosted vaudeville shows originating in San Francisco before it began screening the town's first motion pictures. When a larger movie house, the Gem, was built right next door in the mid-1920s, the older venue began to decline. Efforts to save Thompson's finally got underway seven decades later.

Nestled in the Rocky Mountains of Colorado, the Tabor Opera House (1879) in Leadville is associated with the most famous true romance of the boomtown era. The town, nicknamed "Cloud City," was founded after a gold strike in the area, but came to be better known for its silver mines. Horace Austin Warner Tabor arrived in the district (still part of Kansas Territory at the time) in May 1860. After working as a shopkeeper in Leadville, he became the town's first mayor just before two men he had grubstaked made his fortune. The two miners struck silver at the mine later known as the Little Pittsburgh. Together with the Matchless Mine that Tabor later acquired, this silver strike made him the wealthiest man in the American West. From his newly acquired riches, he lavished nearly $78,000 on his new opera house, designed by architect J. Thomas Roberts.

Of all the melodramas enacted at the Tabor Opera House, the one that captured the most attention took place in the private box occupied by Horace Tabor. This box was the site of the great scandal of the day, after Tabor left his first wife, Augusta, for a beautiful divorcee, Elizabeth McCourt from Oshkosh, Wisconsin. Newspaper accounts of the illicit romance conducted behind the drapes of the private box, appearing internationally, referred to Elizabeth by her more popular name, "Baby Doe." The Tabor story ended tragically when Horace, twenty-four years Elizabeth's senior, died, leaving her a penniless widow in 1899. He had already lost his fortune when the U.S. Treasury went off the silver standard in 1893. Baby Doe is said to have stayed with him to the end, then lived out her remaining years in a shack beside the sealed entry to the abandoned Matchless Mine.

The outcome of the story of the Tabor Opera House has been happier. Threatened with demolition in 1955, the building was rescued when a retired schoolteacher from Minnesota, Florence Hollister, and her daughter, Leadville local Evelyn Furman, purchased the property. Mrs. Furman still maintains the theater, including its old hand-painted backdrops, by offering public tours and occasional shows during the brief summer season in the Rockies.

The discovery of ore in the American Southwest funded the construction of boomtown opera houses in the arid states of New Mexico and Arizona, but it was ranching fortunes that were often behind the opera houses built in Texas during the nineteenth century. Among the half-dozen still operating in the Lone Star State are the Granbury Opera House (1886), its interior updated in the 1970s, and the Bastrop Opera House (1890), with its original tin auditorium ceiling. The Grand Opera House (1891) in Uvalde, Texas, has a pressed-tin frieze running along the upper edge of its exterior brick walls. Its metal dragon weathervane, spinning atop the witch's-cap tower perched over the main corner entry, is only the second to serve at this post. The original firebreather, corroded by a century of Texas weather, now holds a place of honor in the building's first-floor visitor center.

The 600-seat Stafford Opera House (1886) in Columbus, Texas, was built above a bank and a dry-goods store. With its brick exterior, capped by an elaborate cornice, the building stands out in the center of this town, which had to be rebuilt after the

The theater highest in elevation above sea level is the Tabor Opera House (1879) in Leadville, Colorado.

Top: Piper's Opera House (1885) is nestled in a hillside in the town of Virginia City, Nevada.

Above: The corner tower, with a metal dragon on top of its witch's cap, marks the entry to Uvalde's Grand Opera House (1891) in Texas.

original settlement burned in 1836 during the war for Texas' independence. Fifty years after Sam Houston and Mexican General Santa Ana passed through, cattle baron R. E. Stafford hired architect Nicholas J. Clayton of Galveston to design the bank and theater building. The flat-floored upstairs auditorium was slightly modified in the twentieth century, and a replica of the original hand-painted stage curtain was hung.

Another architectural survivor, the Bayview Opera House (1888) in San Francisco, withstood the fires that followed the 1906 earthquake, even with its wooden clapboard exterior. Originally called the South San Francisco Opera House, the building was purchased in 1976 to form part of a community complex known as the Joseph Lee Recreation Center. Among its features, the opera house has a recording studio to the rear of its balcony, filled with equipment donated by the band The Grateful Dead.

In the agricultural regions of central California, the Winters Opera House (1875) and the Woodland Opera House (1896), both near the state's capital city, Sacramento, are also nineteenth-century survivors. The theater in Winters, known for a time as Seaman's Opera House, still has its original wooden stage and a drop curtain dating from 1909 that was found rolled up underneath the stage during refurbishments performed in the early 1990s. Fire destroyed Woodland's first theater in 1892, along with most of the town. In 1913, the present Opera House fell on hard times and closed due to bankruptcy. It sat dormant until 1971, when the Yolo County Historical Society stepped in to prevent demolition of the brick-walled structure. Since 1989, the resurrected Woodland Opera House has been home to the award-winning Resident Theater Company.

Also boding well for theater preservation in California are the recent reclamation of the Sonora Opera Hall (1885) from its days as an auto repair shop, and the healthy state of affairs at the Nevada Theatre (1865) in Nevada City. Ongoing renovation work, begun in the mid-1990s, at the Napa Valley Opera House (1880) further enhances the state's preservationist image.

Elements remaining from the original decor are on display in the Winters Opera House (1875) in California.

Above: The auditorium of the
Woodland Opera House (1896)
in California is one of the
few to have retained this
bowl-shaped section of seats,
a feature popular in many
nineteenth-century theaters
in the American West.

Left: There is no longer a bank
in the building, but the Stafford
Opera House (1886) remains
in business at the center of
Columbus, Texas.

Schieffelin Hall and the Bird Cage Theatre

Schieffelin Hall and the Bird Cage both opened in 1881 but took on very different roles in the history of Tombstone, Arizona. The adobe-walled hall has led a quiet life in comparison with the colorful past of the honky-tonk across town.

Although accounts of the founding of this famous western town differ, the main thrust of the story is clear. Whether the warning came from a great Apache chief or a federal soldier, prospector Ed Schieffelin was told that when he set out to search the Arizona earth for ore-rich rock, the only stone he would find would be his tombstone. What he found instead was the silver vein that led to the founding of the most famous and notorious boomtown in the American Southwest.

The two entertainment halls that survive in Tombstone make a strikingly disparate pair. The Bird Cage Theatre, opened as a hybrid saloon and bordello, quickly became the best-known honky-tonk in America. *The New York Times*, in a profile published in 1882, labeled the Bird Cage as "the wildest, wickedest nightspot between Basin Street and the Barbary Coast." The theater was named for the fourteen "bird-cage" crib boxes, hung seven to a side above the main floor "seating area" (used mainly as a gambling parlor). These infamous boxes, each containing a presiding lady of the evening, were immortalized in a popular song of the day: "She's only a bird in a gilded cage. . . ." As befitted the scene, a French cancan was performed onstage every night, in addition to performances by such theater notables as Lotta Crabtree and Eddie Foy.

Schieffelin Hall was not actually promoted as an antidote to the rowdiness of the Bird Cage and the numerous other drinking establishments in Tombstone, but the building was championed as "a dramatic shrine" in *The Tombstone Epitaph*. The theater, housed within the largest adobe building in the Southwest, was put up by Ed Schieffelin's brother Al. The flat-floored auditorium served as the town's principal meeting hall, as well as a venue for concerts and stage shows. The premiere in June 1881 was called *The Ticket-to-Leave Man*. The title proved to be prescient, for the silver boom in Tombstone did not last even a decade.

Dissent among the miners over wages and the tragic flooding of the mines in 1889 prompted many to desert the town. The Bird Cage was boarded up, while Schieffelin Hall faded more slowly, finally closing in 1917 after its last production, *As You Like It*. Ironically, only after it became a ghost town was Tombstone considered worth reclaiming. Its rebirth as a relic of the Wild West was publicized with the now-famous tag line "The Town Too Tough to Die." The Bird Cage, still scarred by an estimated 140 bullet holes, came back to life as a tourist attraction, promoted as a museum of the American West. Schieffelin Hall was revived to again serve its dual role as the town's municipal and theatrical center. As Tombstone has claimed its place in history, complete with "shootouts" at the OK Corral, it is only fitting that the two old theaters be a part of the show.

Garcia Opera House

This adobe-walled opera house has been in the proud possession of several of the most prominent families in town. Initially, the building was the dream of local miner Juan Nepomocano Garcia and his wife, Francesca, descendants of two of the first families to settle in Socorro. Construction was underway in 1886 when Juan Garcia died, leaving the hall to be completed by Francesca, known around town as Kika. She ran the theater for nearly a decade before selling it in 1895 to Abra Abeyta, another town notable. Renamed the Abeyta Opera House after the sale, the theater was not rechristened as the Garcia Opera House until 1911, when Holm Bursum, a local businessman, acquired the property.

The money to build the opera house came principally from the region's gold and, to a lesser degree, silver and zinc mines. Prior to its construction, the town had lacked any major public gathering spot. Described by the *Socorro Bulletin* that "when completed it will be 124 feet by 42 feet, and will be finished in hardwood," the flat-floored hall was destined to be the site of the town's major weddings, public meetings, and grand balls. A raised stage at the east end was raked slightly, for better audience visibility on those occasions when plays or concerts were presented. But the stage was not the only tilted element of the Garcia Opera House. The long south wall canted outward to support the pitched roof, and although the northern wall was rebuilt, in plumb, some years ago, the massive 34-inch thick wall across the hall maintains its original slant.

Local newspapers reported that one hundred musicians were present opening night, December 1, 1886, to share in the Grand Musical Festival. Before the event was over, the eight hundred seats put up for the show had been cleared to make way for dancing that went on well into the next morning. In quieter years during the twentieth century, the hall has served as a temporary feedstore and as the gymnasium for nearby New Mexico School of Mines, but the primary use of the hall in the mid-twentieth century was for storage.

Then, in 1983, Holm Bursum III, grandson of the former owner, kicked off a fund drive to rehabilitate the Garcia Opera House for theatrical uses. The leaders of society in Socorro again stepped in for their local opera house, by matching the state funds. In January 1985, the hall reopened with performances of *Egad! What a Cad!*, staged by New Mexico's own Madrid Opera House Players. Among the memorabilia discovered during the Garcia's refurbishment was a postcard, unearthed beneath the stage, advertising the arrival of a group direct from Chicago, The Lady Quartette . . . The Society Favorites.

Opposite top: The Garcia Opera House opened in 1886 with a grand festival of music. (Courtesy of Holm Bursum III)

Opposite bottom: Today, the opera house remains a social gathering place in Socorro, New Mexico.

Central City Opera House

The Central City Opera House was built to accommodate its sloping site, just like every other building in this Colorado town.

The major force behind the building of this Rocky Mountain showplace was the predominantly Cornish assembly of mineworkers who had arrived to settle in town during the early 1870s. These miners first helped to collect $25,000 in public subscription monies, then used their skills as stonemasons to assist in the construction work. Part of their motivation came from an understanding that the theater would produce the miners' choral society's shows as regular attractions.

Robert S. Roeschlaub, best known as the architect of the Trinity Methodist Church in Denver, was responsible for the design of the Central City Opera House. He intentionally situated the building above a small creek, in order to use the water to cool the interior during summer performances. The decorative style he adopted for the auditorium has been referred to locally as "Bonanza Victorian." At an elevation of 8,450 feet, the Central City Opera House is reputed to be the second highest theater building in the world, lower only than its fellow state theater, the Tabor Opera House in Leadville.

Among the builders of the Central City Opera House were brothers Will and Peter McFarlane, members of the crew that quarried granite for the exterior walls. Interior work was left primarily to out-of-town experts, including artist John C. Massman of San Francisco. Massman's decorative murals, spanning the side walls of the auditorium, were retouched during a cleanup of the theater in 1987.

The house had a felicitous opening, featuring the music of Verdi and Wagner. The Denver-based *Rocky Mountain News* reported that, for the 756 first-night attendees, comfortable in their hickory-backed chairs, "There's not a bad seat in the house."

News of major silver strikes in Leadville shortly thereafter cast gloom on the fortunes of Central City. The town shrank in size, but managed to hang on until its gold mines finally closed down in the early 1900s. The theater that had proudly served as a regular stop on the Silver Circuit was reduced to showing movies in the early years of the twentieth century. Closed in 1918, the Central City Opera House remained dark until 1930, when Broadway producer Robert Edmund Jones paid a visit to the town. He had come at the request of three women associated with the University of Denver, one of whom, Ida Cruz McFarlane, was married to a descendant of builder Peter McFarlane. The visit led to the rebirth of the venue as home to an annual summer theatre festival in 1932, which ran successfully except during the years of World War II and for repair work in 1982. The first show was *Camille*, with Lillian Gish in the title role.

In recent years, the season has consisted of two operas and an operetta, with all performances in English. The theater is also home to a nationally renowned theater apprentice program, enabling the Central City Opera House to add to its scope. Recently, it established a long-needed rehearsal hall in an old foundry located just uphill from the theater building.

Eureka Opera House

This boomtown opera house faces directly onto U.S. Highway 50, supposedly "the Loneliest Road in America." But things were not always so quiet in Eureka. In the 1880s, the town had five fire companies to protect the more than one hundred gambling houses and honky-tonks in operation. Silver was first discovered in the area in 1864, but the boom was delayed a few years while local smelters were built to enable the separation of silver from the lead-ridden ore.

As the self-proclaimed "Pittsburgh of the West," Eureka found itself in need of a new entertainment hall after a fire destroyed the local Odd Fellows building early in 1880. The Eureka Opera House was completed just in time to hold a masquerade ball in celebration of New Year's Eve that same year. The Eureka Dramatic Club gave the first stage presentation, *Forget Me Not*, on January 22, 1881. The interior of this theater was built with a deeply recessed horseshoe balcony with 64 fixed seats; the main-floor seats were removable, to make way for, as the local paper pronounced, "a good floor for dancing." Renamed the Eureka Theatre in 1915, it featured a steady stream of movies until the late-1950s.

Years of infrequent use followed, until 1988, when a ballot measure was passed, allotting funds for the purchase and rehabilitation of the building as a theater and meeting hall. Thanks to its home county's gold bullion tax, the theater received nearly $2.5 million for its upgrading. Old decor was retouched, an advertising curtain from 1924 was rediscovered and put back in place, and some new facilities for convention gatherings were installed one level below the auditorium floor. The town may be lonely at times, but the renewed Eureka Opera House is a welcoming site, an emblem of a community on the rebound.

The Eureka Opera House counts a Wild West bar among its neighbors on this Nevada stretch of "the Loneliest Road" in the country.

Wheeler Opera House

ASPEN, COLORADO, 1889

The Wheeler Opera House stands today as the grandest reminder of the wealth that silver and gold once brought to the shrewd and the fortunate during the settlement of the American West. The architect of the Wheeler was Harry W. J. Edbrooke, who also designed Denver's Grand Opera House (razed) as a commission for the Silver King of Leadville, Horace Tabor. Edbrooke's client in Aspen was Jerome B. Wheeler, a transplant from Troy, New York. Wheeler was no prospector. He had accumulated his wealth through astute investments in the area silver mines and partial ownership of the Aspen Mining and Smelting Company. He wanted a building that would match the high aspirations of a populace already proud to reside in what the newspapers claimed to be "the first fully electrified town in Colorado."

Wheeler's new building was designed to serve both theatrical and commercial uses, with the auditorium on the third floor, above a street-level bank and second-story offices. Block letters, carved in stone, spell out "BANK" in a small panel located above the first-floor corner entry. This detail, along with the rest of the building's exterior, was made from a peachblow-red sandstone, brought into town from a quarry located in the Territory's Frying Pan Valley. After completion, the multipurpose block immediately assumed the status of a city landmark at the base of Aspen Mountain.

At the time of its opening, the upstairs opera house was hailed throughout the territory as "a model playhouse . . . a perfect 'bijou' of a theatre." In its early years, the Wheeler Opera House was among the major stops on Peter McCourt's Silver Circuit of traveling shows. Shakespeare's plays and the comic operettas of Gilbert & Sullivan were standard fare in Aspen during the first decade of the theater's operation.

It was in the early twentieth century when things began to go wrong for the Wheeler. Declining fortunes, after years of bad management, culminated in extensive damage to the auditorium from two fires of suspicious origin, both occurring in a single week in 1912, during one of which the original proscenium arch was destroyed.

The Wheeler has since undergone several remodelings, and served a number of uses. In 1949, the building was the community house of the Aspen Institute for Humanistic Studies, and was later a home to the Music Associates of Aspen. A busy schedule of live performances and classic film series have drawn crowds back to the theater since its most recent renovation in 1984. Today, the Wheeler Opera House once again exudes the same air of ease and prosperity that marked its glory years.

Above and opposite: The Wheeler Opera House presides over street-level commercial spaces in this block near the center of Aspen, Colorado.

Overleaf: Shutters now keep out the daylight (shown here pouring into the Wheeler's auditorium), adding to the intimacy of this ideally sized top-floor performance hall. (Balthazar Korab)

Revival Halls and the Chautauqua Circuit

TOWARD THE TAIL END OF THE NINETEENTH CENTURY, a diverse collection of utopian societies and quasi-religious organizations established foundation centers and camp meeting-grounds all around the country. The assembly halls and covered amphitheaters built by these groups were not quite full-fledged theaters, but clearly they were not churches either. Public orations and concerts were staged, rather than sermons of a purely religious nature; they were part lesson and part entertainment, directed toward improving public morals and lifting the spirits of those in attendance.

The typological similarities between churches and theaters has historically resulted in an interchangeability of use. While in the twentieth century, former movie palaces in such cities as New York and Chicago have been transformed for religious services, in the previous century, the reverse was more typical. One former religious building, located in Stafford, Connecticut, has been known since 1902 as Memorial Hall (1867). Within the cedar walls of the one-time Spiritualist Hall, the central space now features colorful murals and stencilwork in keeping with nearly a hundred years of theatrical uses.

Thrall's Opera House (1888) in New Harmony, Indiana, is another hall with spiritual origins. The earliest portion of the building was constructed in 1824 as Community House Number Four for the town's founding Harmonist Society, a utopian community established according to the principles of Robert Owen. This dormitory for single men was an adjunct to the town's Workingman's Institute, the centerpiece of this social experiment. The building was eventually remodeled as an open hall in 1856 by the local Thespian Society. The current façade and internal layout, as well as the name of the theater, date to its purchase in 1888 by Eugene S. Thrall. From 1914, the building spent nearly fifty years as an auto repair garage until the State of Indiana purchased it in the mid-1960s, and reestablished it as Thrall's Opera House.

The 1888 exterior of Thrall's Opera House in New Harmony, Indiana, was not difficult to reclaim from its garage days, but the interior renovation was a major repair job.

147

The history of the chautauqua movement and its associated summer camp meetings around the United States has been covered in numerous books. This grassroots movement, named for its founding lakeside institution in Chautauqua, New York, evolved in the last quarter of the nineteenth century. Its stated goals included the greater spiritual, social, and cultural advancement of society as a whole. The wellspring operation in western New York inspired the creation of an estimated two hundred permanent chautauqua sites. The Chautauqua Amphitheater (1893) at the flagship site in New York is a simple timber-framed structure of great expanse, with seating for 5,500 on its pewlike benches. In its peak years, the chautauqua circuit included stops at many of its 12,000 temporary venues. The orators, performers, and social activists of this movement spent entire summers on the circuit, appearing mostly in open-air amphitheaters,which could fan out to seat thousands.

A handful of the old chautauqua sites around the country still go by the name, operating as summer retreats, with their theaters still in use, including the wooden halls of South Auditorium (1884) in Lakeside, Ohio, and the rebuilt tabernacle hall of the Fountain Park Chautauqua (1898) on the outskirts of Remington, Indiana. The Chautauqua Hall (1889), once known as Chautauqua-by-the-Sea, in Pacific Grove, California, has served in recent decades as a gymnasium and the town's Cub Scouts hall.

In 1994, fire struck the Mount Gretna Playhouse (1892), also known as the Little Theatre in the Woods, destroying most of this wooden showplace of the South Central Pennsylvania Chautauqua campgrounds. Portions of the entry pavilion survived, to form the starting point for the reconstruction of the amphitheater. A new twelve-sided roof covers the polygonal space below, its 710 seats about three hundred fewer than the earlier structure contained. A summer stock venue since 1927, the playhouse reopened for the 1995 season.

Intended primarily for use in fair weather, the halls of summer camp meeting sites were usually rough in construction, rarely more elaborate than the wooden huts and canvas tents that housed camp attendees. Those that remain are the exceptions. But if the typical chautauqua theater was less than elegant, as a group they have a notable legacy: they are the precursors of the many summer music festival halls that dot the country today.

Fire destroyed all but the box office at the front of the Chautauqua Playhouse (1892) in Mount Gretna, Pennsylvania, in 1994. By early spring 1995, the new auditorium was nearing completion, with a portion of the original box office wing tucked under the new roof. (Courtesy of Gretna Productions)

Ryman Auditorium

Only Tennessee residents and America's preservationists are likely to think of this building as the Ryman Auditorium. A far wider audience knows it better as the Grand Ole Opry House. Broadcast live from the stage of this one-time revivalist tabernacle once a week from 1943 until 1974, the Grand Ole Opry Show attracted fans as fervent as any who attended the old revival meetings. This downtown landmark reverted to the Ryman name after the final Opry season in 1974, when the show was transferred to a new site on the outskirts of Nashville, as part of the $15 million Opryland, U.S.A. complex.

The first home of the Grand Ole Opry has a curious past. It originated with a change of heart experienced by a local riverboat captain, Thomas Green Ryman. In 1885, so the story goes, Captain Ryman accompanied some friends to a revival meeting in town. Their intent was to heckle the principal speakers, but Ryman converted on the spot. Meeting again three years later with the instrument of his conversion, evangelist Sam Jones, the captain decided to raise a tabernacle to serve as a permanent site for future gatherings. Construction began the following year for a building that opened in 1892 as the Union Gospel Tabernacle. Architect A. T. Thompson chose a Gothic Revival design, popular in late Victorian times, with a polychrome red-brick and white-stone exterior, and several rows of lancet-arched, stained-glass windows.

Sam Jones returned to Nashville in 1904 to deliver the eulogy for Ryman, at which time the tabernacle was renamed the Ryman Auditorium. In the years that followed, many stage luminaries appeared here, including Sarah Bernhardt in a 1906 production of *Camille*. The following year, both President Theodore Roosevelt and temperance spokeswoman Carrie Nation delivered public addresses from the Ryman stage. The next decade brought war bond rallies and Billy Sunday revivals to the hall. Finally, in 1943, the Grand Ole Opry Show premiered.

Radio station WSM started broadcasting live shows in 1925, and opened its studios for public attendance in 1939. The shows were then moved to the city's War Memorial Auditorium, and next to the Ryman, when even a (then-steep) twenty-five cent admission failed to keep the crowds from overflowing the broadcast venue. Over the three decades of Grand Ole Opry, patrons of the Ryman were treated to such stars as Hank Williams, Patsy Cline, and Loretta Lynn. Roy Acuff launched his standard "Wabash Cannonball" during a live broadcast on the Opry stage. In 1963, the radio station finally purchased the building, rechristening it the Grand Ole Opry House. Ten years later, the show was moved and the building abandoned.

It took another twenty years to get the Ryman back on its feet. Following centennial celebrations for the building in 1992, an $8.5 million renovation was begun, and the Ryman Auditorium was born again. The onetime "Mother Church of Country Music" is now a living memorial to country music in its dual role as a performance venue and a museum.

Opposite: Ryman Auditorium, later famous as the "Mother Church of Country Music," is located not far from the center of Nashville. (Courtesy of the Ryman Auditorium)

Overleaf: During its years as host for Grand Ole Opry radio broadcasts, the Ryman stage was graced by all the stars of country music, replacing the hell-fire evangelists who preached here when the building was still a religious tabernacle. (Courtesy of the Ryman Auditorium)

APPLAUSE

The Temple

A giant octagon of wood, the Temple rises like a huge green-and-white mirage from within a quiet stretch of pines near the coast of southern Maine. The building is no more miraculous considering it took less than two months to build in the summer of 1881. The interior, with its great web of timber trusswork overhead, serves only to increase the wonder at the speed at which the building rose. Architects Dow & Wheeler designed the Temple for a modest fee of $27.50. Portland builder James Bickford and his crew first took up the plans on June 6, 1881, and had the building finished for its dedication on August 2. A bell tower just east of the Temple was erected the following year. Together with Porter Hall and Jordon Hall, two nearby structures built early in the twentieth century, the Temple and bell tower form Temple Square, the formal name for this woodland quartet.

The Temple occupies a quiet spot a short walk from the town beach. Some ingenious alterations to the timber trusswork cleared the way for movie projection at the Temple.

A plaque above the main entry doors to the Temple proclaims it as the centerpiece of the Ocean Park Association, which was "Founded 1881 by Charter from the State of Maine. To a group of Free Baptist Ministers and Laymen." The Temple has played a central role ever since in the annual ten-week assembly seasons, which are interdenominational.

In addition to assembly gatherings, the Temple hosts various musical events, including concerts performed on the twenty-six-rank pipe organ. In the late 1980s, the program superintendent, Richard F. Burns, revived an old chautauqua tradition, Illumination Night. Held in early August, the annual celebration in Ocean Park is recognizable by the appearance of Japanese lanterns strung around the Temple Square grounds. A summer film series has proven a popular new tradition. The first film showings at the Temple, in 1919, led to the most significant alteration of the building to date. Originally, a thick central post rose from the center of the polygonal floor to the base of the lantern that caps the structure. Today, a suspended web of iron flanges supports the lantern, forming a cat's cradle for the truncated post, its bottom cut away so as not to interfere with audience sightlines. Aside from this change, the Temple remains true to its original and remarkable construction.

The Great Auditorium

With seats for more than 6,500 spread across the main floor and the surrounding gallery, this is a building that deserves its grandiose title. The deep, open expanse of the interior is presided over by the laminated wooden beams that span the auditorium roof. A steel framework supports the three-sided gallery. The architect of the Great Auditorium, Fred T. Camp, did not neglect the exterior of the building either. The triple-towered front is impressive and somewhat fanciful, facing the Atlantic Ocean just a short distance away. In spite of its grandeur, the total construction cost of $69,612 seems remarkably low, even for its day.

The green space stretching between the Great Auditorium and the beachfront is now known as Founder's Park. It was on this site, in the summer of 1869, from which the auditorium can mark its beginning. Ten families had assembled there for the purpose of "rest and religious fellowship." One man, Dr. William B. Osborn, had selected the spot for its grove of trees and the relative scarcity of mosquitoes and it was he who named the place Ocean Grove. The following winter, an organization composed of thirteen ministers and thirteen lay members created the Ocean Grove Camp Meeting Association (no relation to the architect), and held its first official assembly the following summer.

During its early decades, the Ocean Grove Association erected a number of small halls, of which only the Bishop James Tabernacle of 1877 and Thornely Chapel of 1889 have survived. For the large assemblies held in the late nineteenth century, only partial cover was provided. Typically, a simple frame structure was erected, using tree boughs for roofing. Not surprisingly, camp attendees complained about the makeshift construction, especially when boughs continued to drip long after the cessation of the frequent summer showers.

To fulfill the need for a permanent, drier meeting hall, a crew of approximately thirty workers met for an informal groundbreaking on December 2, 1893. A three-day inauguration commenced the first day of July the following year. Still serving as the centerpiece of its founding organization, the Great Auditorium has weathered its years well.

Above: The ironwork underneath the balcony of the Great Auditorium is an exception in the otherwise all-wood building.

Opposite: The front face of the Great Auditorium sets an impressive example for the beachfront settlement of Ocean Grove, New Jersey.

Chautauqua Auditorium

The founders of this chautauqua defined their mission as "the drawing together of people for discussion, entertainment, and recreation." They could not have produced a more powerful drawing card than this auditorium and the surrounding 26-acre Chautauqua Park. Set at the base of Boulder's famous slope-faced Flatirons, the park was the brainchild of a group of Texas educators looking for a place to establish a summer learning institution. The site was chosen after a $20,000 bond issue to purchase the Rocky Mountain foothill property was passed by the town's five thousand residents. The Texans' desire to mix entertainment with education motivated the building of the Auditorium. The immense wooden structure was in place by Independence Day 1888, for the opening of what, for a time, was known as the Texado Chautauqua in honor of the founders. Renamed the Boulder Chautauqua soon after, the initial number of public buildings and residential cottages steadily increased until 1918, when the last major public building, the Community House, opened.

From the start, the Auditorium was the heart of the community. The original design, by architects Kidder & Rice of Denver, rose in fields previously used to grow alfalfa. The structure was completely assembled in just sixty days. The only significant alteration to the interior of the building since that time was the removal of the original firwood bandshell at the front of the hall. In 1905, the Boulder City Council approved an expenditure of $425 to build "a proper stage." Shortly thereafter, 600 new "opera chairs" were installed to replace some of the original wooden benches, the hardness of which produced the income of a boy stationed near the entrance, calling out, "Cushions! Five cents!"

The first performers at the Chautauqua Auditorium were believers in so-called Brimstone theology, who may well have preferred the older, less comfortable seats for their audience. Foremost among regular speakers was Billy Sunday, who appeared numerous times between 1909 and 1931. In 1907, a new "flicker-free" Vitagraph projection system brought the movies to the Boulder Chautauqua. From that season on, two or three movies were screened each year prior to the Depression.

At present, the buildings and grounds of Chautauqua Park are the property of the City of Boulder. A not-for-profit organization, the Colorado Chautauqua Association, oversees park operations and produces summer events at the Auditorium. In a recent poll conducted by *Inside Performance* magazine, the country's top performing artists included the building as among the ten best entertainment halls in the nation. Perhaps the most appropriate compliment was paid by musician Michelle Shocked. While onstage at the all-wooden Chautauqua Auditorium, she reportedly exclaimed, "This is what my pick must feel like when it falls inside my guitar!"

The bare-bones interior of the Chautauqua Auditorium is more than compensated for by its fanciful front and spectacular setting, just below the Flatirons.

Community Halls and Library Theaters

SECULAR COUSINS TO THE TEMPERANCE HALLS AND CHAUTAUQUA theaters of the late nineteenth century were the multipurpose community halls and library theaters. Many of these buildings were planned as gathering places for immigrant communities, such as the Czech Opera House (1901) in for the town of Wilson, Kansas. And German gymnastic societies, called Turn Vereins, often incorporated a stage at one end of their athletic halls. Turner Hall (1874) in Galena, Illinois, is among the survivors of this type. (The name Galena derives from a compound of lead sulfate that was the source of the town's early prosperity.) The limestone exterior of this city-owned theater has an appropriate yellowish cast. The auditorium had to be rebuilt in 1926 following a fire that permanently cost Turner Hall its central cupola. A different kind of Turn Verein reconstruction occurred downriver from Galena, where the former St. Louis Turn Verein was transformed into luxury apartments in the early 1980s.

Another Czech-founded social assembly space occupies the upstairs realm of the CSPS (Sokol) Hall (1887) in St. Paul, Minnesota. American Sokol organizations, created to maintain Czech cultural traditions, date back to the parent assembly founded in Prague in 1862. In another part of Minnesota, transplanted Finns built the Onnen Toivo Temperance Hall (1896) in Cokato. The name of the hall is said to translate to "Hope for Happiness." Its purpose was to further the spiritual life of this predominantly Lutheran settlement. The wooden hall was home to a mix of dramatic productions, band concerts, and boxing matches over the years, but is currently open only once each year for an annual observance of its founding.

Both educational and athletic activities took place at the Athenaeum (1898) in Indianapolis, Indiana. This brick and terra-cotta building was designed with a Renaissance Revival look by the firm of Vonnegut & Bohn, headed by the grandfather of writer Kurt Vonnegut, Jr. The interior of the performance hall was remodeled in 1989 by the American Cabaret Theatre to serve as its home theater.

A number of educational institutions opened their own public theaters to broaden their audiences. The 160-seat theater at the back of the Starr Institute Building (1862) in Rhinebeck, New York, was used temporarily as a bowling alley before being converted to a movie theater. A short distance downstate, the two sons of Matthew Vassar, Poughkeepsie brewer and founder of Vassar College, developed their own facility, the Vassar Brothers Institute (1883). Their two-building campus included a public theater that was

The theater sits within one of the pair of buildings that originally made up the Vassar Brothers Institute (1883) in Poughkeepsie, New York.

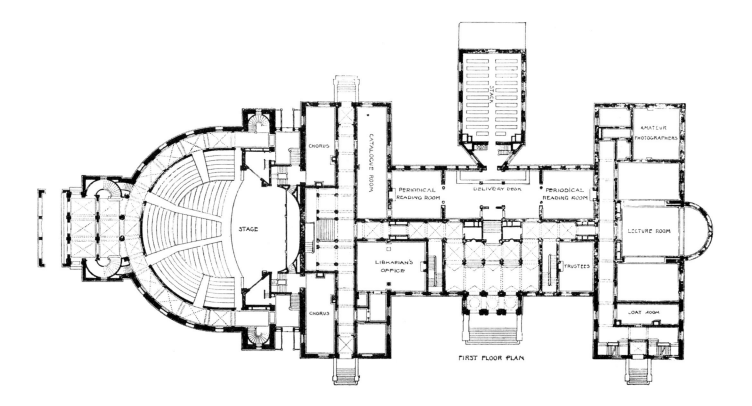

FIRST FLOOR PLAN

Above: Carnegie Music Hall
forms part of a library-theater
combination opened in the
Oakland district of Pittsburgh,
Pennsylvania, in 1895. (Carnegie
Library of Pittsburgh)

Opposite top: The Czech Opera
House in Wilson, Kansas, was
started in 1900, but not opened
until early in the next century.

Opposite bottom: The fire
station is a twentieth-century
addition, clad in similar
stone, to Turner Hall (1874)
in Galena, Illinois.

used primarily for dramatic productions and illustrated travel lectures. Now part of the Cunneen-Hacket Cultural Center, the hall presents dance recitals and movie screenings.

Pittsburgh steel magnate Andrew Carnegie was a prolific builder of educational institutions and public libraries around the country. The major complexes he funded are in the communities around Pittsburgh, which were home to the workers at many of his business operations. The grandest of the theater spaces attached to one of his institutions is the Carnegie Music Hall opened in 1895, as part of the Carnegie Institute and Library in the Oakland district of Pittsburgh. The architects for this venue, the firm of Longfellow, Alden & Harlow, also designed another library complex a few miles up the Allegheny River, near Carnegie's Homestead steelworks. The Homestead Library, with its barrel-vaulted music hall, was dedicated in a speech by Carnegie himself in 1898.

Reminiscent of city hall opera houses, some towns managed to combine virtually all of their public services in a single building. The Stoughton City Hall in Wisconsin originally had all its town offices, along with the police and fire department, on its first floor, and the public library on its second. The 650-seat City Hall Theater (1901) occupies the upper reaches of the building atop the library. In Michigan, the Vermontville Opera House (1898) is raised only a few steps above the sidewalk level, with the library partially visible below.

Unlike the social halls and the theaters attached to public institutions, most library theaters were entirely public venues. As long as library visitors who wished to read in peace were undisturbed, the adjoining performance spaces played host to a wide variety of theatre, dance, or music performances. These theaters were no wallflowers architecturally despite their scholarly associations, but instead comprise a remarkably ornate collection of showplaces. The fact that they were often built as memorials to wealthy benefactors explains at least in part their elaborate designs.

163

Above: Stoughton City
Hall in Wisconsin
originally had the town
library on its second floor.

Opposite: Atop the library,
the City Hall Theater
(1901) occupies the
building's upper floors.

St. George Social Hall

The St. George Social Hall sits on a rise at the north end of this Utah town.

A sign freshly painted in early 1995 announced the impending rebirth of the St. George Social Hall, to be known as the Pioneer Center for the Arts. A much smaller plaque, near the hall's lower entrance, tells of the building's past: "The Opera House served as the cultural center of the community from 1875 until the early 1930s. The original 'T' shaped building seated 300 persons." The text goes on to note the hall's most unusual feature: "A mechanically adjustable sloping floor afforded an excellent view of the stage." Although the floor mechanism is no longer functioning, the turnscrews that permitted this transformation of the Social Hall's auditorium are still on view in the basement of the building. Also still visible are the dowel-filled openings on the main floor that were originally designed to hold special "wooden slat pegs." The purpose of the pegs was to secure the seats when the auditorium floor was cranked into sloped position for a theater performance. The seats were easy to remove when public meetings or ballroom dances were scheduled.

Aside from its overscaled frontispiece, the exterior of the Social Hall is noteworthy for its variety of building materials. The foundation was built of dark gray lava rocks, while the walls of the raised hall were made of adobe bricks covered with a coat of stucco. The intervening pedestal level was clad with red sandstone quarried from the rugged cliff formation looming just north of the building and the center of town. Now under the auspices of the City of St. George, the Social Hall once again can host a full range of community events.

Tivoli Turnhalle

DENVER, COLORADO, 1882

The buildings once collectively known as the Tivoli Brewery, including the rejuvenated Turnhalle, stand tall on the southwestern fringe of Denver's central business district. A large portion of the converted brewery now serves as a student union for neighboring Auraria College, with other areas converted into retail outlets, a public library, and a multiplex cinema. When ongoing renovations are completed, the Turnhalle is expected to serve as a conference room, in addition to its role as a public venue.

The oldest portion of the building complex was constructed in 1870 by Moritz Sigi to serve as his Colorado Brewery. Sigi's Hall, built alongside the brewery building, was the forerunner of the Turnhalle as the first meeting place for the West Denver Turn Verein. In 1879, Max Melsheimer bought out Sigi, and renamed the place the Milwaukee Brewery. It was during Melsheimer's management that the complex was expanded to include the brewery's central brick tower, a retail store for the workers, and, in 1882, the Turnhalle. Officially designated the West Denver Turnhalle, the 700-seat theater was designed by Harrold W. Baerresea, in conjunction with the chief architect for the brewery additions, F. C. Eberly.

Money troubles beset Melsheimer in 1901, forcing him to yield his interest in the brewery to his previously silent partner, John Good. It was Good who rechristened the operation the Tivoli, in homage to the famous amusement park in Copenhagen, Denmark. On his orders, the buildings were repainted in the orange, white, and sky-blue color scheme that became a Tivoli trademark. Beer continued to be produced under the Tivoli banner as late as 1969, featuring such brands as Aspen Gold and Mile-Hi Beer.

The Turnhalle stayed in operation until it suffered major damage during flooding in 1965. Thirty years later, it became the last of the major spaces to be overhauled for reuse. Ongoing major work involves a reconstruction of the wraparound gallery and a re-creation of a proscenium arch for the rock-maple stage, the sole intact feature remaining from the original Turnhalle interior. Aside from its coat of whitewash, the exterior of the hall is little changed from 1882. A plaque noting the inaugural year and the full name of the structure is visible high up on the north wall.

The Tivoli Turnhalle (1882) is the last of this former south Denver brewery to be brought back into use.

Mechanics Hall

The pipe organ and its decorative frame fill the east wall inside Mechanics Hall.

From its inception, this hall was envisioned as a training center for young artisans and craftsmen, called "mechanics" in the parlance of the era. The Worcester County Mechanics Association was formed in 1842 under a leadership composed of local mill owners and merchants. A decade later, this organization decided to construct a new facility, to include a lecture hall, concert arena, and an open exhibition space for the display of industrial products. Architect Elbridge Boyden was contracted to design the new Mechanics Hall. Boyden placed the building's main auditorium on the third floor, one flight up from Washburn Hall, the lecture space named for association member Ichabod Washburn, who first suggested that the complex be built. The upper hall became far more popular than ever anticipated by Washburn and his colleagues, featuring such stars of the day as John Philip Sousa, Enrico Caruso, Mark Twain, and Artur Rubinstein. The hall also served as a boxing and rollerskating arena.

The centerpiece of the main auditorium in Mechanics Hall is an 1864 Worcester organ, produced by the Hook Brothers Company of Boston. This instrument is reputed to be "the oldest unaltered four-manual organ in the Western Hemisphere." Its pipes form the dominant feature of the eastern interior wall. Changes to the interior have been minimal over the years, with the most dramatic alteration occurring in 1977, when a glass-walled entry lobby was constructed at what had been the rear of the building. This addition is a marked departure from the classically inspired main street façade, currently painted a chocolate brown.

Mechanics Hall no longer hosts educational sessions for young mechanics, and no exhibitions chart the industry of the past century, but as Worcester's center for public meetings and performance events, its importance is undiminished.

Library Theatre

W A R R E N ,   P E N N S Y L V A N I A ,   1 8 8 3

At the time of its opening on December 3, 1883, the Struthers Library Building housed not only the public library and a theater, but also retail spaces and the central Warren post office. The building was a gift to the town from local industrialist Thomas Struthers; as soon as construction was completed, Struthers transferred the deed for the building to Warren County Judge William D. Brown and a board of six trustees.

The new theater was equipped with sixteen sets of scenery and a collapsible wooden floor that could be unfolded above the main-floor seats for conversion to a ballroom. In the three decades that followed the opening-night production of *Iolanthe*, performed by the Walker Opera Company, the theater remained primarily a playhouse. Changes started happening in 1916, when the town library constructed a new building all its own. The post office followed suit one year later. In 1919, the Library Building trustees hired Warren & Wetmore of New York, the architects of Grand Central Station, to remodel the theater interior. For approximately the same amount—$80,000—it had cost to put up the original building, the auditorium was updated to its present appearance. The price tag included installation of a theater organ to be used as accompaniment for plays and silent films. Talking pictures arrived in 1929, when the Warner Brothers' movie chain assumed control of the Library Theatre until 1966. When the next managing company departed in 1980, a group that came to be known as the Friends of the Library Theatre brought the showplace back under local control, and began to gradually refurbish the building.

Among the spaces most true to the original design is the old Library Room, located in the front half of the second floor. Cast-iron columns, each decorated with a filagreed "S" for Struthers, are evenly spaced around the room, supporting the twenty-foot ceiling. However, the theater space is more movie house than playhouse in appearance, but at least an echo of its former elegance remains.

Industrialist Thomas Struthers funded construction of the Library Theatre. The auditorium was updated in 1919, but the exterior is largely unchanged. (LHAT)

172

Mabel Tainter Memorial Theater

The Mabel Tainter Memorial has stood rock solid for a century, unchanged even by twentieth-century soot.

The Moorish-derived ornamental scheme of this memorial theater, including broad expanses of hand-carved, gold-painted woodwork, was produced by a little-known architect, Harvey Ellis. Remarkably, this jewel of a theater and the adjoining library were completed for only $105,000—the carved sandstone exterior alone is grand enough to have used up the entire budget.

The namesake of the building, Mabel Tainter, was the third child of Wisconsin lumber baron Andrew Tainter and his second wife Bertha. The couple and their daughter were prominent members of the town's Unitarian Society, organized in 1888 by the Reverend Henry Dotson Maxson. It was the reverend who conceived the idea of a memorial building, following the death of Mabel at age nineteen, apparently from a ruptured appendix. The building was intended "to contribute something toward the intellectual, social, and moral advancement of the community." Deeded at the time of its completion to the control of Dunn County, the building is also home in perpetuity to the Unitarians.

Spiritual and entertainment needs were accounted for by the theater space; intellectual pursuits by the library. The main reading room, as extravagantly appointed as the rest of the building, still has its original mahogany reading table and a fireplace built of Mexican onyx. The sandstone for the exterior was taken from the Dunnville quarry by rail to the Red Cedar River, then floated on barges to Menomonie. The stone was carved on site and set in place by a crew of nearly one hundred stonecutters, the majority of them transplanted Scots. The ship's prow headstone, erected in front of the exterior stair landing, pays honor to Andrew Tainter and his early employment as a steamboat captain.

Among the many original features still in place in the Mabel Tainter Memorial Theater are the Italian marble floors in the lobby and a number of stained-glass windows with uplifting messages worked into their designs. The theater still operates as a hemp house, running lines off a wooden pin rail; its circular water radiators are still functional. The original $5,000 Steere & Turner tracker pipe organ, shipped from Springfield, Massachusetts, was restored in 1957 after a period of dormancy.

The interior decor has been little altered over time. The stencilwork patterns on the walls and ceiling were all painted by hand directly onto wet plaster. The artists used a mixture of calcimine paint, dry pigments, and egg whites. The original house drapes, imported from India and Italy, include a butterfly curtain that can be manually raised and lowered in wing formations from a catwalk above the stage.

Two pieces of sculpture are not original to the theater. The busts of Andrew and Bertha Tainter, presently atop pedestals alongside the opposing main-floor boxes, were moved in the 1960s from the main reading room. They replaced the original pair of busts, which depicted two other Unitarian notables, Ralph Waldo Emerson and Senator Charles Sumner. It seems only fitting that a theater given in a daughter's name include her generous parents.

Gilded woodwork designs draw the eye inside the Mabel Tainter Memorial Theater, Andrew and Bertha Tainter's gift to the town of Menomonie in memory of their daughter. Sculpted busts of each of the parents sit atop pedestals along the opposing main-floor boxes.

Cumston Hall

Neither theater benefactor Charles McLaughlin Cumston nor architect Henry Hayman Cochrane was a native of Monmouth, yet both became strongly attached to their adopted hometown. After graduating from local Monmouth Academy, Dr. Cumston left to take a position at English High School in Boston, where he stayed for twenty-six years before retiring from the headmaster's job to return to Monmouth. In 1899, he offered the Town of Monmouth a bequest of $10,000, to be matched by tax revenues, for the purpose of building a new town hall. The architect preferred by Cumston to design the building was the multitalented Cochrane, already heralded in the region as "the Maine Leonardo." The Augusta-born Cochrane had married and moved to Monmouth a few years earlier, in the midst of a career devoted primarily to art and building decoration. Prior to the Cumston Hall commission, he had never had complete control of an architectural project.

It was Cochrane who campaigned for the inclusion of a library as part of the town hall building, on top of which he added a small but highly ornate theater. Cochrane supervised the team of local carpenters who crafted the wooden structure, with its array of milled columns, clapboarding, and fancy shingle patterns. Cochrane's own artistry is best seen in the fresco panels of the theater's dome. The faces of the various frescoed figures are reputed to be modeled after those of local citizens, including Mrs. Cochrane and the couple's daughter. The plasterwork decor of the proscenium arch and the opera boxes, as well as the stained-glass windows of the Cumston Hall stair tower, were also designed by Cochrane. And, in a final display of versatility, Cochrane composed the music for the building's dedication ceremony and conducted the orchestra.

The premiere at Cumston Hall proved to be the beginning of the theater's long tradition of theatrical and musical productions. Since the late 1960s, the hall has been home to the Theatre at Monmouth, a repertory theater group that shares the building with the Cumston Public Library Association.

The play is still the thing at Cumston Hall.

Haskell Opera House

One look at the plaque on the front of this building is sufficient to alert visitors they have encountered an extraordinary situation. Two names are listed: "La Bibliotheque Public et La Salle D'Opera Haskell" and "The Haskell Free Library and Opera House." This is a public building that serves two separate publics, residing on different sides of an international border. Thus, the building is open to citizens of both Canada and the United States. And although the entry to both the main-floor library and the Opera House, located one flight up, are on the American side of the border, the international boundary line bisects the library reading room on the diagonal, so most of the books are shelved in Canada. Upstairs, the majority of the seats are above American soil, but performances are staged in Canada.

Construction of this binational venue did not get underway until October 1901, but this is clearly a nineteenth-century opera house in its tastes and aspirations. The metal plaque notes that the building "testifies to the late Victorian belief in the intellectual and moral benefits of education and the arts." The theater interior was intended to be a scaled-down version of the old Boston Opera House (razed in the middle of this century). A pressed-tin ceiling makes a shallow vault overhead; a balcony curves beneath, its front decorated with plasterwork cherubs strumming mandolins. A painted trellis, its vines in full bloom, extends across the top of the proscenium, ending at each side beside a long-tressed nymph in peaceful repose. The exterior of the building is equally nostalgic, its Queen Anne styling executed in yellow brick with granite trim.

The building was conceived as a memorial to prominent Derby Line resident Carlos F. Haskell by his widow Martha Stewart Haskell. She and her son donated the combined library and theater to citizens of the two adjacent towns. The principal architect was James Ball of Rock Island, Quebec, while construction was overseen by Nate Beach, a Vermont veteran of the Civil War. The Haskell Opera House opened on June 7, 1904, with the Columbia Minstrel Troupe presenting the musical comedy *The Isle of the Rock*. A full house of 648 was equally delighted with the show and the theater, despite the absence of padding for their seats.

A more serious shortcoming—no adequate fire egress—forced the Haskell to close in 1993, because while Vermont fire codes required a new balcony fire escape to be provided, this kind of drastic alteration is expressly forbidden in Quebec by the province's Cultural Property Act of 1992. A section of wall covered by one of the reclining nymphs is a possible casualty of the proposed alteration. The library and the theater are both incorporated in Vermont, but the threatened section of wall is unquestionably on the Canadian side. Resolution of this issue was still pending in early 1997. As a result, this venue for everything from Gilbert & Sullivan operettas to country music hoedowns is closed indefinitely. The library, however, continues in service, offering books and magazines in both French and English.

Opposite top: At the Haskell Free Library and Opera House, the library door faces America, while the balcony overlooks Canadian soil.

Opposite bottom: The reclining figure at the upper left of the proscenium arch may be lost in the construction of a required fire exit.

Victorian Playhouses

DURING THE LAST TWO DECADES OF THE NINETEENTH century, a particularly graceful collection of theater buildings rose in cities all around the nation. Even as they acknowledged the debt they owed to the playhouses and opera houses of Europe, American theater architects adapted and expanded upon these precedents until their buildings took on undeniably local styles.

One example is the Rockport Opera House (1891), which stands on a bluff above the rugged coast of Maine. The whitewashed exterior has the look of an old meetinghouse, though its sternness is enlivened by the multicolored glass panes of the transom window above the entry doors. The interior is another world: on one hand, it resembles an English music hall, but with its fancifully decorated horseshoe balcony, wooden wainscotting, and painted stencilwork on its upper walls, there is also a definite American flavor to the design. For all the beauty of the Rockport theater, it is the Portsmouth Music Hall (1878) in New Hampshire that has staked a claim to the title, "the handsomest provincial theater in New England." It too has an ornamental balcony front set on a horseshoe curve. Double-deck opera boxes on either side of the stage feature a neo-Palladian look, with trumpeting cherubs at their peaks. Sadly, the frescoes of the ceiling dome remain concealed under a layer of paint applied early in the century when the Music Hall underwent its conversion into a movie house.

The main façade of the Music Hall (1885) in Tarrytown, New York, is Queen Anne style with a polychrome brick and stone, featuring brickwork corbels at the bases of the corner towers. Local chocolate manufacturer William Wallace hired architect Philip Edmunds to build the Music Hall. A remodeling conducted in the years when Art Deco was all the rage has left Edmunds's original interior design somewhat muddled. However, a proscenium mural, measuring 60 by 15 feet and painted in the manner of the Hudson River School, was left undisturbed by the alterations.

Two Pennsylvania towns with major playhouses from the period are Meadville, with its Academy Theatre (1885; originally the Academy of Music), and Towanda, home to the Keystone Theatre (1886), which opened as Hale's Opera House. The Academy was a gift to the town from local philanthropist Earnest Hempstead. Meadville newspapers hailed the playhouse as "a new and beautiful Temple of Amusement, a credit to the city and an honor to its proprietor." In Towanda, a carved stone panel set into the brick street façade, above the Keystone marquee, is a reminder of the original Hale's name.

In Kentucky, one Victorian venue, the Lexington Opera House (1887), arose after its predecessor had burned down. And despite the fact that the original Washington Opera

Fine detail is a hallmark
of Korner's Folly (1880) in
Kernersville, North Carolina.

Opposite: The sign says "OPERA," but the Washington Opera House rebuilt in 1898 in Maysville, Kentucky, is really a playhouse.

Above: A portion of the town's Down East harbor can be seen behind the Rockport Opera House (1891) in Maine.

House of Maysville, Kentucky (1851) was built using public subscription monies raised by the town's Washington Fire Company and included a fire bell, weighing 1,285 pounds, above the opera house's main façade, fire claimed the building in January 1898. A new Washington Opera House was completed by the end of the same year. Another fire in 1930 necessitated a partial reconstruction of the opera house, whose main fare by this time was movies. The Maysville Players purchased the building in 1965 and have remained in residence ever since.

Unquestionably the most unusual Victorian-era playhouse in the country was built as part of a true *play*house. Now called Korner's Folly (1880), this brick building occupies the plot of land popularly known as Cupid's Park in Kernersville, North Carolina. Where the exterior indicates just two full stories and a garret underneath the steeply pitched roof gables, the interior is actually a three-dimensional jigsaw puzzle, holding twenty-two miniature rooms on seven levels. The playhouse is tucked inside the attic. The doll-house array of rooms was designed and built by Jule Korner, the son of a clock salesman who founded this North Carolina town after emigrating from Germany. Jule was a photographer and an artist, whose other claim to fame was as creator of the popular handpainted bulls used in the 1880s to advertise the Blackwell Tobacco Company's Bull Durham products.

The house folly was initially planned as a studio office and carriage house. Eventually, it was reconfigured to include a ballroom, the various playrooms, and the attic theater. Work was completed on Easter Monday in 1880, at a total cost of around $200,000. It was likely it was this figure that prompted Jule's cousin Nathaniel to give the place the name "Folly." The theater still has its original stage curtains and reflectors left from the old kerosene footlights. The murals along the inclined walls look as though they were painted on sheets of parchment that are now curling at their edges. Over time, the Korner's Folly playhouse came to be used as "a little theater" for the surrounding community. In this spirit, a citizens group purchased the building in the 1970s to ensure it would remain available for use.

The steep attic roof makes for interesting spaces inside the playhouse theater of Korner's Folly (1880), Kernersville, North Carolina.

Not every playhouse of the period was so fanciful, although the variety of these venues was astonishing. What these period theaters serve collectively to illustrate is a maturing of theater design taking place at that time in America. The architectural treatments developed for these playhouses indicate that their designers were confident in their abilities to dazzle and delight contemporary theatergoers.

Symphony Hall

ALLENTOWN, PENNSYLVANIA, 1899

The building today known as the Allentown Symphony Hall had origins at once more humble and more grandiose than is suggested by its sober stonework exterior. Known variously as the New Markethouse or the Central Market Hall when it opened in 1896, it initially was display space for livestock and farm produce. The original design included a stone tower and an imposing pediment, both of which were removed during alterations to the building in 1920.

The theatrical life of the hall dates to 1899, when the New York firm of J. B. McElfatrick & Sons was called in to redesign the interior as a playhouse. Thanks to the efforts of this talented firm, the former marketplace possesses the quiet elegance and ideal proportioning that were to become McElfatrick trademarks. No single feature of the design stands out, but the overall effect is supremely enjoyable.

The altered space reopened as the Lyric Theatre on October 10, 1899, with a production of the stage drama *Frederick the Great*. No stranger to politics, the theater hosted Theodore Roosevelt and Woodrow Wilson, each while in office as President. In a lighter vein, at least three of the Marx Brothers came to Allentown to perform at the Lyric. Renamed Symphony Hall, restoration work began in 1995, with a few test panels, located along the opera box fronts, which were cleaned and repainted. Plans are to refurbish the auditorium along the lines of its 1899 appearance.

Opposite: The plasterwork decor of Allentown's Symphony Hall was built to designs by J. B. McElfatrick & Sons of New York.

Right: The Symphony Hall exterior was likely just as impressive when it served as a farmer's market hall from 1896 to 1899.

Grand Opera House

Meridian's Grand Opera House is considered by theater experts to be the oldest surviving example of the more than two hundred theater designs created by the firm of J. B. McElfatrick & Sons, possibly the most prolific theater builders in history. The Meridian opened on December 17, 1890, with *The Gypsy Baron*, featuring the music of Johann Strauss. At the time, the Grand Opera House had twenty-five full sets of scenery, a remarkable number, all the work of the Chicago firm Sossman & Landes. The auditorium filled the upper floors of the six-story Marks-Rothenberg Building, a mercantile office block.

Meridian was a prosperous city in the late nineteenth century, due in part to its role as the hub of five intersecting railroad lines. The Grand Opera House benefited greatly from this situation, as the city became a major stop for every vaudeville show and Shakespearean troupe traveling between Atlanta and New Orleans. In the early years of this century, the city hosted more than one hundred visitors a night, many of whom found their way upstairs to the Grand Opera House, where they were treated like royalty. Ushers at the Meridian Grand delivered boxes of candy to ladies in the better seats every night at intermission.

As the century progressed, the fates were not so kind to the Grand. Currently, the interior is considerably worse for wear, although the old cherrywood wainscotting and the floral-motif wallpaper original to the theater are still visible. Plasterwork cherubs and the gilded faces atop the stacked opera boxes all remain in place. Little used since 1927, when it ended service as a movie house for the Saenger Theater Company, some efforts were made in the 1990s to bring the place back to life. Still badly in need of a complete overhaul, the Grand nevertheless is testimony to a glamorous past.

Nearly a century separates these two views of the Grand Opera House.

Fulton Opera House

LANCASTER, PENNSYLVANIA, 1852

This building, first known as Fulton Hall, was erected on a site occupied during the colonial era by a stone prison, infamous after the last of the Conestoga Indians were massacred there in 1763 by the Paxtang Boys, a group of frontier vigilantes. The frontier had moved well beyond Lancaster by the 1850s, when local businessman Christopher Hager decided to build a new hall to be used as theater and community center.

Opposite: This arrangement of the Fulton Opera House auditorium dates to changes made in 1904. (LHAT)

Architect Samuel Sloan, one of the most prominent practitioners in the country, was hired to design Fulton Hall. Among the unusual features of his design was the inclusion of a shooting gallery on the fourth floor, directly above the hall's auditorium. A carved cedar statue of namesake Robert Fulton, sculpted by Hugh Cannon, assumed its place in a niche over the theater entry two years after the building was completed. An apocryphal story associated with this belated installation tells of workmen so frustrated with their foreman that they considered having him petrified and put in Fulton's place.

Records indicate that Fulton Hall opened in 1852 with a violin concert given by a Norwegian master named Ole Bull. The name of the hall was changed to the Fulton Opera House after major alterations were made to the auditorium in 1873. A second balcony was added during a second round of revisions in 1904. By the 1920s, the Opera House was screening movies, and remained in this role for about forty years.

The Fulton Opera House was one of the first American theaters to be fully reclaimed from its movie house status for live performances. Successful efforts begun by new owners in 1963 to rehabilitate the theater ultimately led to the Fulton being named a National Historic Landmark six years later. As a not-for-profit institution, the Fulton Opera House has since become home to the Lancaster Symphony Orchestra, the Lancaster Opera Company, and the Actors' Company of Pennsylvania.

Above: Robert Fulton was removed from his niche during renovations of the Lancaster, Pennsylvania, showplace carried out in 1995–96.

Goodspeed Opera House

The initial efforts to save the Goodspeed in the late 1950s serve as the symbolic first shot fired in the battle to save America's nineteenth-century theatrical heritage. Scheduled to be torn down in 1958, the hall was given a reprieve when the Goodspeed Opera Foundation was formed to halt the demolition. In the following years, this rescue team lobbied private and state government sources for funds to restore the Opera House. Finally rehabilitated in 1963, the theater reopened with a production of a revival of the 1918 musical *Oh, Lady! Lady!*, a work by Jerome Kern, P. G. Wodehouse, and Guy Bolton.

The reopening marked a new dawn for the Goodspeed, as it inaugurated an experimental policy of musical theater production. The opera house became the primary incubator for a new generation of American musicals. The list of Broadway hits first performed at the Goodspeed Opera House is testimony to the wisdom of the theater's benefactors. The top three musicals launched in East Haddam were *Man of La Mancha* (1966), winner of five Tony awards; *Shenandoah* (1974), winner of two Tonys; and *Annie* (1977), which won an astounding seven Tonys. The theater itself has received two of these cherished statues; it was awarded a special Tony in 1980, "for outstanding contributions to the American musical," and a second in 1995 "for distinguished achievement in regional theatre."

Along with these relatively recent successes, the Goodspeed Opera House possesses a colorful past. Jebez Comstock served as general contractor for the construction of this building, first known as Goodspeed Hall. William H. Goodspeed, a shipbuilder with a love for the theatre, paid for the wooden structure with profits from his shipyards. The "occasional entertainments" hosted at the theater often featured performers brought into East Haddam just for the occasion, transported by steamboat from as far away as New York City, and delivered directly to the Goodspeed's own dock on the river running alongside the theater. The close ties to Manhattan's Broadway district are just as strong today. With its award-winning production policy, the Goodspeed Opera House richly deserves its current title as "the main address for the American musical."

Above: The sign just below the cupola notes 1876 as the year the Goodspeed Opera Hall, as it was first known, was completed. (Courtesy of the Goodspeed Opera House/LHAT)

Opposite: The Goodspeed has its own dock on the river.

Academy of Music

With its well-preserved air of Victorian charm, this former playhouse (now a movie theater) is unique among its American counterparts: a year after its opening, the Academy of Music was deeded to the Town of Northampton, to be owned and operated thereafter as a municipal theater. All operations are overseen by a board of directors that includes permanent seats for the mayor of Northampton and the president of nearby Smith College.

The Academy of Music was created as an altruistic measure by a local philanthropist, silk tycoon H. R. Lyman. In the early years following Lyman's gift to the town, the principal tenants were the Northampton Players, a local repertory theatre group. By the turn of the century, touring shows had become the staple attraction. One of these shows starred Jenny Lind, the actress who gave Northampton its nickname, "The Paradise of America."

William Brocklesby, an architect from Hartford, Connecticut, designed the Academy of Music in accord with design tenets of Romantic Rationalism. As such, the purpose of each portion of the building had to be clearly identifiable by its external shape. Directly in back of the Academy's landscaped forecourt is a grand ceremonial entry block, behind which rises the main body of the theater. Looming at the far end of the site is the immense shed-roofed form of the stagehouse.

All exterior ornamental flourishes are concentrated on the entry block façade. From a base of carved stonework, the upper stories rise with a facing of buff-colored brick. The cresting pediment is flanked by sections of carved stone balustrading. Terra-cotta accents are sprinkled liberally along the surface of the façade, including a series of plaques bearing the names of well-known classical composers.

The musical motif is carried throughout the interior. Various instruments are depicted in the stained-glass windows set in the transoms above the doors to the inner lobby. A conductor's stand holds the place of honor at the front of the orchestra pit in the Academy's 1,040-seat auditorium. The chief decorative effects of the Academy of Music are elaborate double-deck opera boxes on either side of a golden picture-frame proscenium, and the fancy-fronted balcony, supported by a row of wooden columns with gold-painted shafts.

There have been few changes of any note to the look of this showplace. Sometime in the first half of this century, a flat-faced, neon-trimmed announcement board was built directly above the main entry doors designed to sit flush with the rest of the façade. Currently, the Academy of Music plays host, on occasion, to locally produced dance and theatre, in addition to the regular movie screenings. Lyman's gift from more than a century ago remains a beloved institution, prized by townspeople as a theater of their own.

The Academy's interior decorations are most ornate around the opera boxes and the picture-frame proscenium.

Colonial Theatre

Opposite: Plaster cherubs watch over the seats from the box and balcony fronts, inside Boston's Colonial Theatre.

Overleaf: A mural fills the surface of the sounding board above the Colonial Theatre stage.

Since its opening December 20, 1900, with a production of *Ben Hur*, the Colonial has retained its leading role as a major venue for live theatre in Boston. In its early years, it hosted *The Ziegfeld Follies*, produced by legendary New York showman Florenz Ziegfeld. The *Follies* that played at the Colonial more recently were the work of Harold Prince and Stephen Sondheim. A who's who list of actors played here over the intervening years, including Fanny Brice, Fred and Adele Astaire, Paul Robeson, Laurence Olivier, and Carol Channing. No theater has proven better suited to stage the great dramatic productions and musical highlights of the twentieth century than the Colonial.

Noted Boston theater architect Clarence Blackall created some particularly ornate decor for the mirror-lined inner foyer and nearly every square inch in the Colonial's auditorium. Built at the turn of the century, the Colonial serves as a bridge between the playhouses of the late Victorian era and the glitzy movie palaces that followed in the 1920s. The notable artwork in Blackall's design includes the ceiling fresco, executed by Herman Schladermundt, who had worked on the Library of Congress in Washington, D.C. Inside the Colonial, the artist incorporated various allegorical figures in the decor, symbolizing earthly virtues and the high arts.

Through years when many of the nearby venues in Boston's theater district fell on hard times, the Colonial has never been in serious jeopardy. Rich in both appearance and history, the Colonial Theatre is today what it was originally intended to be: "A monument to the taste of New England and a credit to the City of Boston."

Folly Theater

K A N S A S   C I T Y ,   M I S S O U R I ,   1 9 0 0

The Lighted Ball signals an opening night at the Folly Theater. (© Mary S. Watkins 1997/Courtesy of Folly Theater)

The Folly has had a colorful—some might say checkered—history. Originally the Standard, it was a burlesque house; later it was known as the Century and Shubert's Missouri, before finally being named the Folly in 1941. Through all the name changes, the theater has wowed its patrons, from the opening production in 1900 of *The Jolly Grass Widow*, through its final days as an X-rated movie house in 1973, with Miss Chesty Gabor live on stage to complement the film screenings. Other disparate notables over the years included the Marx Brothers, Chief Blackhawk, the Kings of Hokum, and an attraction suggestively billed as "The Beef Trust." One early employee of the theater was Frank James, brother of the notorious outlaw Jesse James. During the 1920s and 1930s, the Shubert Organization brought its National Players to town for performances of plays ranging from Shakespearean tragedies to the works of Eugene O'Neill, starring the likes of Humphrey Bogart, Fanny Brice, and Shirley Booth.

The Folly Theater was designed by Kansas City's best known architect, Louis Curtiss. His other buildings in town included the more elaborate Willis Wood Theater, demolished long ago, and the Boley Building, one of the first metal-and-glass curtain wall buildings in the world. Curtiss was considered an eccentric, sporting white suits and shoes, and often wearing a monocle, but his belief in the powers of the Ouija board and the occult did not seem to have had any discernible effects on his design for the Folly.

The most striking exterior feature of the theater is the central Palladian-motif window grouping. The ornamental trim of this and other elements of the façade appear to be cut stone, but are in fact made of galvanized iron and zinc. One special feature, unique to the theater, is the Folly's Lighted Ball. Measuring a full 3 feet in diameter and studded with bare bulbs, this electrified globe is illuminated and hoisted up its corner pole for every evening performance.

Entrance lobbies, just inside the front doors, are both new and modified spaces meant to resolve the problem of the formal jumble of lobby spaces, which once included the base of a staircase rising directly to the "peanut gallery" at the back of the uppermost balcony. The original layout of the theater included two balconies; currently, there is only one large balcony. The older wooden balconies were lost to fire in the 1920s.

Where burlesque once reigned supreme, musical and dance performances have become the norm on the Folly stage. After Chesty's final curtain calls in 1973, the Folly was scheduled to be demolished. Instead, a campaign was launched by a not-for-profit organization that drew on contributions from Kansas City citizens to purchase the old theater for a half-million dollars. Much more was raised from local contributors over the decade that followed the sale, enabling the Folly board to renovate the existing structure and build a new support wing for theater operations. By 1981, the Folly had a full-time manager at its helm, and the Lighted Ball was being raised with regularity once again.

Grand Opera Houses and Concert Halls

ERY FEW OF THE NINETEENTH-CENTURY THEATERS BUILT in America that were called grand opera houses ever had the resources to stage a grand opera. And even if they had, full-scale operatic productions were not yet a popular art form for much of this still-young country. Nevertheless, the best of our theatrical venues were still grand, at least in their decor. By contrast, the top American concert halls of the late nineteenth century were relatively spartan in design, but in their capabilities to host superb musical performances, they were a match for any halls in the world.

Among the handful of theaters known for both acoustics and architectural brilliance, the Troy Savings Bank Music Hall (1875) ranks at the top of the list. Renowned twentieth-century conductor George Szell once said that the Music Hall has the finest sound of any theater in the country. The auditorium, which rises a full 60 feet, is visually as well as acoustically impressive. And though the interior decor is far from ornate, the organ pipes towering above the back of the stage and the colorful stencilwork panels around the top edge of the side walls delight the eye. Main-floor seating is supplemented by two shelf balconies at the back of the hall and triple-tiered boxes along both sides. The most astonishing fact about the Savings Bank Music Hall is that this vast interior volume is suspended between a great banking hall below and an immense attic space overhead.

New York City architect George B. Post handled the exterior design of Troy's Music Hall with forthright massing and precise detailing. Post later designed such landmarks as the New York Stock Exchange (1901–04) and the Wisconsin State Capitol Building (1904–07) in Madison. Only thirty-four years old when he received the commission to design the Troy Savings Bank building, Post's reputation as a talented architect was assured with its completion.

Among the vast number of American theaters to sport the title "opera house," a pair of southern belles warrant some attention. The Grand Opera House (1884) in Macon, Georgia, began its existence as the Academy of Music. At the time of its opening, it was lauded in the local press as "a model of elegance and a triumph of good taste; the prettiest amusement house in the south." Modifications to the building, begun in 1902, led to its reopening as the Grand Opera House three years later, with an office block

Edward Francis Searles commissioned the construction of the Music Hall (1899) in Methuen, Massachusetts, just to house this massive German pipe organ. (J. David Bohl)

rising above the theater's outer lobby area. The Springer Opera House (1871) in Columbus, Georgia, was remodeled during roughly the same period as its counterpart in Macon. Its red-brick exterior was little changed, but its auditorium was realigned at a 90-degree angle to the original layout. The new configuration of opera boxes and balconies made the refurbished Springer look like a close cousin to the Macon Grand.

Another theater that underwent major alterations, and a name change as well, is the Lyric Opera House (1894) in Baltimore, Maryland. Opened as the Baltimore Music Hall, the original auditorium is largely intact, but a modern lobby was added in 1982, the stage was overhauled the following year, and new seats were installed the year after that. Still, enough of architect T. Henry Randall's interior remains to show the magnificence of his nineteenth-century design. Each of the decorative panels, set into arched openings along the sidewall arcades, is inscribed with the name of a classical composer. And, in a bow to Maryland history, a cartouche bearing the Calvert family coat of arms is included above the center of the stage. Opened on Halloween night in 1894, the Lyric has been in operation ever since, except during periods of modification.

In the older centers of the Northeast, two of the most venerated concert halls in the country remain fully active. New York City's best-loved performance space, Carnegie Hall (1891), seats 2,800 across five levels. Two continuous rows of opera boxes, a dress circle, and an upper gallery curve from the sides around the back of the hall, above the orchestra floor seating, enclosing patrons in a bowl of sound. In contrast, Boston's Symphony Hall's (1900) 2,625-seat auditorium is rectangular, designed by the revered New York firm of McKim, Mead & White.

Despite the disparity in their shapes, both halls are highly regarded for their acoustics (with Carnegie Hall once again in good graces following removal of a layer of concrete inadvertently left underneath the new stage during renovation in the early 1990s). Many theater experts consider Symphony Hall to be the birthplace of the modern science of acoustics, and a central factor in the worldwide acclaim of the Boston Symphony Orchestra.

Carnegie Hall was designed by William Burnett Tuthill as philanthropist Andrew Carnegie's gift to Manhattan. It was originally known simply as the Music Hall. The name Carnegie Hall was adopted three years after the opening, to distance the venue from the vaudeville-type entertainments performed in most "music halls" of the day, as opposed to the highbrow fare of the more serious named "concert halls."

Among Andrew Carnegie's fellow patrons of the arts was a former interior decorator, Edward Francis Searles, from Methuen, Massachusetts. Searles was working in San Francisco when he met the widow of railroad baron Mark Hopkins. Twenty-two years older than Searles, Mary Frances Sherwood Hopkins (another Massachusetts native, from the town of Great Barrington) eventually proposed marriage to him. He accepted in 1887 and, upon her death four years later, inherited the entire Hopkins fortune. With this bounty, he returned home to Massachusetts and erected his own

Above: The Troy Savings Bank Music Hall (1875) in New York was an early commission in the oeuvre of master builder George B. Post.

Opposite: The Methuen Memorial Music Hall is situated alongside the Spicket River in Massachusetts.

grand concert hall. Now known as the Methuen Memorial Music Hall (1899), this imposing 65-foot brick building stands alongside the Spicket River, the principal waterway of this New England milltown. The building's height was determined by Searles' plan to transfer to the Music Hall a massive concert organ that had been removed from the old Boston Music Hall. The organ was manufactured in 1863 by the E. F. Walcker firm of Ludwigsberg, Germany. Searles hired English architect Henry Vaughan to plan the concert hall around the eventual installation of the huge instrument. A plaque located high on the north exterior is evidence of Searles' dream; it reads: "The Serlo Organ Hall, Anno Domini 1899." Sadly, Searles died in 1902, seven years before the organ was fully installed.

Although no American theater or concert hall ever has acquired the cachet of Garnier's l'Opéra de Paris or La Scala in Milan, the Philadelphia Academy of Music and the Auditorium Theater in Chicago are worthy challengers. And the designs for the majority of American theaters built in the late 1800s were of a consistently high quality, replacing Old World expertise with a homegrown inventiveness.

A pair of Georgia showplaces, Macon's Grand Opera House (1884) and the Springer Opera House (1871) in Columbus, inside and out, were both remodeled in the first decade of the twentieth century.

Two of the Northeast's best
regarded highbrow venues
are Symphony Hall (1900) in
Boston, and Carnegie Hall
(1891) in New York City. (LHAT)

Steinert Hall

Boston's Steinert Hall
looks elegant even in decay.

This small recital hall must be ranked as one of the most unusual anywhere in the world, by virtue of its location alone, ensconced beneath a multistory commercial office building. Steinert Hall is as soundproof as a vault, with its base level a full 35 feet below the sidewalk frontage on Boylston Street. The architect purposely designed this as a subterranean hall, to seal it off from the clip-clop of passing horsedrawn carriages on the cobblestone street. While this measure was effective acoustically, it eventually ended the hall's days as a public performance space. Concerns for the safety of patrons and players in the event of a fire forced management to shut down the space in the 1940s.

Today, well into its retirement from public life, the hall serves mainly as a storage area for the piano showroom located on the main floor of the building above. However, because of its still-remarkable acoustics, the hall does host occasional recording sessions. Ironically, the Steinert has been deemed an ideal venue for the late twentieth-century practice of digital sampling, with the notes from ultramodern instruments bouncing off the comparatively ancient walls.

Beyond its acoustic properties, Steinert Hall is remarkable for its architecture. Unfortunately, visitors must use a flashlight to see what remains of the former grandeur of the lobby, located at the bottom of a staircase just inside the building's main entrance. Passing into the performance hall is not unlike entering a damp natural cavern. The space opens up, however, after moving from under a short shelf balcony. Opposite the entry, at the front of this oval hall, is a niche set into the end wall that holds a platform stage, just large enough for a string quartet or a solitary grand piano. The backdrop for this stage is decorated only by a blank medallion and plasterwork door moldings, framing an opening just wide enough for a piano to pass through.

Long bereft of chairs, the main floor area of Steinert Hall has only pegholes to indicate where rows of seats once were placed within the oval interior. Despite the tomblike atmosphere that now prevails, much of the clarity of the original design for the hall remains visible. Certainly enough is left to recognize that Steinert Hall stood briefly as a masterpiece equal in spirit to the best works of the Italian Renaissance.

Granger Hall

Built as a private concert hall attached to the home of Ralph Granger and his family, this small wooden building, eighty years after its construction, was transplanted to its current location in National City, California. A music lover and a collector of antique violins, Granger was a Colorado silver baron who had moved to the San Diego area in 1890. Irving Gill, the architect of the hall, came to town two years later, after working in Chicago for the renowned firm of Adler & Sullivan. Gill would go on to establish an international reputation, responsible for such masterworks as the La Jolla Women's Club (1912–14) and the Dodge House (1914–16) in Hollywood.

Prior to building the hall, Granger had developed a habit of inviting touring musicians to stay at his house and give private concerts in the main salon. With the completion of the concert hall in 1898, the salon was turned into an entry foyer. This space and the hall were all that survived when a fire consumed the Granger home in 1906. There was never any attempt made to rebuild the house, leaving Granger Hall an unused orphan. As years passed, the hall took on an air of mystery, becoming known to locals as "The Sleeping Beauty of Paradise Valley." In 1963, one of the Granger grandchildren undertook a partial restoration of the hall, but it wasn't until 1978 that the hall was rescued, when the South Bay Historical Society moved the building to its present site.

Granger Hall holds its own even next door to a used car lot. The interior blends the look of a grand salon and a small recital room.

The shingle exterior and the oversized wooden brackets—inserted to support the hall's low-hipped roof—indicate that Gill borrowed architectural effects from such sources as the English Arts and Crafts Movement and the Shingle Style, once popular in the northeastern United States. To bring light inside this wooden concert hall, Gill punctured the long sidewalls with rows of tall oval windows.

The enclosed recital hall measures 32 by 100 feet. The walls splay outward slightly, away from the stage, while the floor slopes gently down toward the front of the hall and can hold as many as 200 seats. These two features were designed to enhance both the acoustics and sightlines. The hall's original pipe organ is gone, but its wooden grill-work remains intact, as does a collection of some six hundred piano rolls for a player piano. Intricate stencilwork can still be seen high along the sidewalls, serving to frame the artwork overhead, where a 75-foot-long mural runs the length of the hall's main ceiling cove. A ring of cherubs circle the central figure of Euterpe, the Greek muse of Music. Now primarily a venue for small public concerts, Granger Hall has stayed faithful both to its muse and to the man who had it built.

Academy of Music

When this building was first proposed in 1852 by a group of local businessmen, it was envisioned as this country's answer to the great opera houses of Europe. A national competition to design the hall was won by a hometown firm, the partnership of Napoleon Le Brun and Gustavus Runge. After being awarded the commission, Le Brun made a European pilgrimage, visiting La Scala and other halls, before returning to finalize plans for the new Philadelphia theater. The configuration of the auditorium is the element of the Academy most closely tied to the European models. Mimicking La Scala's interior, semicircular tiers of seats are stacked to curve around this near-cylindrical volume of space. Rows of cast-iron Corinthian columns around the upper-tier rims give the impression of private boxes, a design widely used by European theater designers. In Philadelphia, however, no such divisions were actually made, permitting better sightlines for everyone in attendance.

Decorative touches in the Academy of Music's auditorium are most elaborate near the opera boxes, which are stacked at either side of the stage. Kneeling heroes of mythical proportions take shape in plaster atop the upper boxes, in support of the auditorium ceiling. From the ceiling hangs the city's grandest chandelier, which is encircled by a fresco attributed to artist Constantin Keyser. Other ceiling murals by Karl Heinrich Schmolze portray allegorical figures representing the Fine Arts.

The Academy of Music first opened its doors for a grand ball held in January 1857. A month later, the opera *Il Trovatore*, by Giuseppe Verdi, had its American premiere at this theater. An insertable hinged floor also enabled the Academy of Music to host nontheatrical events, and President Grover Cleveland took advantage of this feature to hold his wedding dinner here. The leveled auditorium was also the site of the city's first indoor football game, played between the University of Pennsylvania and nearby Princeton.

As home to the Philadelphia Orchestra, one of the premier musical groups in the world, the Academy has always maintained an air of great dignity. The theater has changed so little that, in 1994, it was used as the set for razed New York City venues in the movie version of the Edith Wharton novel *The Age of Innocence*. The scenes were thoroughly convincing in their historical accuracy, thanks in no small part to their architectural backdrop.

Opposite: The tall and stately interior of the Philadelphia Academy of Music is closely modeled on European halls.

Below: Cast-iron columns surround each gallery to support the next row above.

Grand Opera House

Designed to house the temples of the state Masonic chapter, the Grand Opera House graces downtown Wilmington with its magnificently proportioned cast-iron face. The well-balanced rhythms of this main façade are in full accord with the predominant French Second Empire style, which architect Thomas Dixson adopted for the exterior. Three tiers of engaged columns mark off these rhythms, stacked in support of the building's richly embellished Mansard slate roof.

The cornerstone for the Grand Opera House was laid April 20, 1871, and the building was open in time for Christmas that year, with three days to spare. The extensive cast ironwork of the main façade was created by the Royce Brothers Company of Philadelphia. Each section of this metal exoskeleton was lifted into place, bolted down, and then painted to suggest the appearance of chiseled marble.

A chandelier was intended to hang from the center of the auditorium ceiling, but the idea was scrapped in favor of smaller fixtures at the ceiling corners. This change made room for a trompe l'oeil oculus, to provide patrons with an imaginary glimpse of the sky. The frescoed ceiling surrounding the oculus was painted by the Kehrweider Brothers for $1,800, with an additional $200 for the design. A reporter for the *Delaware Gazette* wrote of "the dome of cerulean blue ornamented with gilt stars," and listed by name and domain the eight muses depicted in the areas around the oculus.

The entertainment presented at the Grand has proven as diverse as the ceiling muses. The early years featured stage shows, public lectures, and musical concerts, including one played in 1878 on a new Edison phonograph. However, what opera there was at the Grand was mainly comic. Things changed in the first decades of the twentieth century when first vaudeville, then movies became the mainstay of the theater. By 1921, the conversion to a movie house became fully apparent when a wide, electric marquee, spelling out "GRAND," was hung in front of the theater.

What this sign also signaled was the start of a long decline in fortune for this once-grand venue. Preservation activity finally got underway in 1971 following a costume ball, in honor of the building's one-hundredth birthday, sponsored by the Victorian Society in America. A not-for-profit organization brought the Grand Opera House back to life just in time for the country's bicentennial celebrations.

Above: The Grand Opera House sits comfortably along Wilmington's downtown pedestrian mall. (LHAT)

Opposite: The Grand was renovated shortly after its 100th birthday.

Grand 1894 Opera House

GALVESTON, TEXAS, 1895

Both the interior of the opera house and an attached hotel, which served to shield the theater interior from street noise, were completed in 1894, with this date carved in stone atop the building's horseshoe-shaped entry arch. However, the Grand Opera House narrowly missed opening that year, coming out on January 3, 1895, with a performance of the drama *Daughters of Eve*. Newspaper reviews were glowing, for the building if not the performers: "The most important dramatic event in the history of the city took place last evening when that new and magnificent Thespian temple, the Grand Opera House, was formally thrown open to the public."

The hotel's seventy-five rooms were let on what signs promised was "the European plan." The theater, by contrast, was an all-American venue. Frank Cox of New Orleans was the designer for the Grand, and he created an auditorium that unquestionably lived up to its title in both scale and ornamentation. Cox even handpainted the house drop curtain with his allegorical vision of "Sappho and Her Companions."

Following its successful start, however, the Grand Opera House was treated badly by both Man and Nature. A major storm devastated Galveston and the theater in 1900. Both stage walls collapsed, and the hotel lost its upper floor and crowning cupola. The theater was reconstructed, but later lost most of its original interior details in the 1920s and 1930s when the Grand became a movie house.

Its present status is the result of renovation efforts begun in 1979 by the Galveston County Cultural Arts Council, whose goal was not a full-scale restoration but something far more elusive: to recapture the flavor of the theatergoing experience as it was during the first years the Grand was open. Preservation specialist Killis Almond, Jr., working out of San Antonio, in conjunction with preservation heavyweights Hardy Holzman Pfeiffer Associates, mined local archives for guidance in restoring the interior to its nineteenth-century essence.

The result is an "interpretive restoration" (a term attributed to architect Malcolm Holzman). This approach has proven successful in restoring the atmosphere if not the precise architectural details of the 1894 interior. Cox's original stage curtain was replicated, and newly carved limestone blocks, copies of the original stonework, were used to reconstruct the exterior entry arch. This interpretation is remarkable, in places, even magnificent. The colorful decor is eyepopping without being overdone. Features such as the Grand's dozen rebuilt opera boxes, staggered six to a side, are among the finest architectural creations in an American theater of any age.

Above: Entrance to the Grand 1894 Opera House is by way of this carved-stone horseshoe arch.

Opposite: The 1979 restoration replicates the original house curtain designed by Frank Cox. (Van Edwards/LHAT)

Cincinnati Music Hall

CINCINNATI, OHIO, 1878

Composed of nearly four million bricks, the Cincinnati Music Hall was erected during a year-long race against time to open for the city's annual May Festival in 1878. The principal backer for the new building, Reuben Springer, had been present in 1877 when rain falling on the tin roof of the previous venue, Saenger Hall, had disrupted that year's celebrations. Subsequently, Springer put up $125,000 to match an equal amount contributed by local citizens to build this imposing (and, presumably, weatherproof) festival site. In tribute to his generosity, the main performance space in the Music Hall complex was named the Springer Auditorium.

As designed by Cincinnati architects Hannaford & Proctor, the Music Hall combined three separate buildings under one very elaborate roof. The northern hall originally was used as a sporting arena, but has since been converted to serve as a rehearsal hall and scenery storage shop. The southern sector of the complex was the primary industrial exhibition center for Cincinnati, before the modern convention center opened in 1967. The spacious auditorium at the heart of the Music Hall seats more than 3,600 ticketholders.

The Music Hall was completed on time for the May Festival, built over foundations

from the city's Orphan Asylum of 1844. The original interiors were largely undecorated, including the Springer Auditorium, whose gallery and proscenium arch were not constructed until 1895.

In contrast, the Music Hall exterior was never considered plain. With its sky-piercing towers and polychrome cladding of brick and stone, highlighted by a great rose window on its eastern face, it is more likely the Music Hall would have been mistaken for a church. Over time, the building has become home to the city's top cultural organizations, hosting ballet, opera, and symphonic performances. This enormous nineteenth-century creation, once described facetiously as styled in "Sauerbrauten Byzantine," was named a National Historic Landmark in 1975.

Auditorium Theater

CHICAGO, ILLINOIS, 1889

The Auditorium Theater Building fills an entire block at the southwest corner of the Chicago Loop. Its sheer bulk is a major reason this venue is still around, having twice been spared from demolition by the prohibitive cost of carting away its heavy limestone cladding. No longer threatened by the forces of urban renewal, the building finally received its due in 1975 when it was designated a National Historic Landmark.

Architects Adler & Sullivan had already built several theaters in Chicago and at sites throughout the Midwest when lawyer Ferdinand W. Peck hired them in 1885 to redesign the interior of Chicago's Interstate Industrial Exposition Building. Peck, president of the city's Opera Festival, wanted to turn the cast-off exposition building into a temporary performance hall. The commission provided an ideal opportunity for the architects to try out certain ideas that would later influence the design for the Auditorium Theater. Peck offered the architects this second commission shortly after the test run of the Opera Festival proved successful. The new theater was to be the centerpiece of a seventeen-story tower planned to include a 400-room hotel, 136 offices and stores, a small recital hall in the space above the main auditorium, as well as offices for the Adler & Sullivan firm. The tower, capped by a U.S. Signal Service weather station and an astronomical observatory, rose to an elevation of 270 feet above street level, earning the Auditorium Building status as the tallest of its day in Chicago; it was also the most massive piece of architecture in the modern world, weighing in at 110,000 tons.

Both the building as a whole and its tenant theater are generally considered to be the product of Adler's engineering genius combined with Sullivan's seemingly endless capacity for ornamental invention. The tower was a major challenge for Adler. Searching for a way to counteract the severe load imbalances created during construction, Adler strategically placed a pile of pig iron and brick at its base. This scrap was then gradually removed as the tower grew to assert its own load. In spite of the fact that the entire exterior wall is load-bearing, the architects had to use cast- and wrought-iron elements extensively, to develop an interior structure capable of supporting the complex room arrangements of the multipurpose commercial block.

Nowhere is this inner structural system more critical than where it supports the ceiling of the Auditorium Theater. Here, a widening succession of elliptical plaster

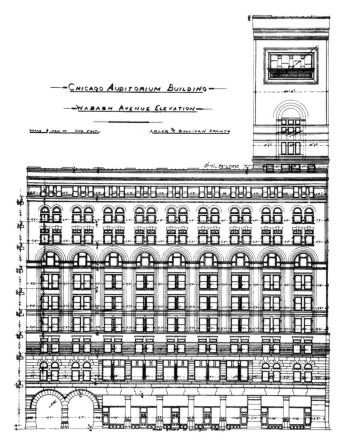

arches are suspended from a rigid iron skeleton. The telescoping character of the arches serves to funnel the sound to the upper reaches of the theater with astonishing fidelity. Each arch also masks a complex set of mechanical systems. So-called gilded beehive ventilation domes, manufactured to Sullivan's specifications, alternate along the length of each arch with unique bare-bulb light fixtures. The lightbulbs for the Auditorium were custom-manufactured by the Thomas Edison Company. The pentagonal base of each nipple-tipped carbon filament bulb was painted olde gold to match the overall color scheme of the decor. The hemispherical beehives, also colored to match, serve as vents through which to heat and cool the theater. The Auditorium was even designed with a rudimentary air conditioning system, fed by air channeled over huge blocks of ice placed in subgrade chambers.

With 4,237 seats, the Auditorium Theater became the largest enclosed performance hall to date, although by lowering sets of panels concealed above both the upper and lower galleries, the size of the vast interior can be reduced for more intimate presentations. Additionally, a sectional floor, stored in the basement, can be positioned above the orchestra level seats to create a flat-floored banquet hall with seating for 600, a feature put to use even before the building was completed. Under a temporary roof, the theater was host to the Republican National Convention in 1888. Benjamin Harrison emerged as the party's presidential candidate, and returned, victorious, to dedicate the Auditorium Theater in December 1889. The floor was also assembled to make an arena for "Chicago ball," an indoor variety of softball. During World War II, the Auditorium became a USO center, and bowling lanes were temporarily installed onstage.

The end of the war marked the beginning of a hiatus for the Auditorium Theater. In 1946, the recently established Roosevelt University purchased the entire building and converted it into classrooms, lounges, library space, and administrative offices. Nearly all of the Auditorium Building was back in use by 1948, but rehabilitation of the auditorium itself was beyond the financial means of the university.

Thus, the theater remained dark until 1960, at which time the Auditorium Theater Council was created by the university's board of trustees, and given the task of finding a way to resuscitate the theater. Under the guidance of the trustees, working with architect Harry Weese, the Auditorium Theater was restored and reopened in 1967. Given a second chance, this architectural tour de force has reassumed a major role in the entertainment life of Chicago. With the loss of the Chicago Stock Exchange Building, the Auditorium is now the sole survivor of Adler & Sullivan's major works in the city.

Two views contrast Chicago's Auditorium Theater as it appears today and as it might have appeared in 1889, with the architects and their wives in attendance along with the cream of midwestern society. (LHAT)

Alphabetical List of Theaters by State and City

Organized in the following order: State/City/Theater Name (Year Opened)/Address/Number of Seats/Owner as of 1995/Use/Original Architect/Builder

Alabama

Fort Payne
Fort Payne Opera House (1890)
510 Gault Avenue North, 35967
450 seats, 3 levels
Landmarks of DeKalb County, Inc.
Plays and concerts

Arizona

Tombstone
Bird Cage Theatre (1881)
East Allen Street, 85638
185 seats, box "cribs"
Privately owned
Museum
William J. Hutchison, architect/builder

Tombstone
Schieffelin Hall (1881)
4th and East Fremont Streets, 85638
200 seats, 2 levels
Masonic Lodge and City of Tombstone
Cultural center and town meetings

Arkansas

Van Buren
King Opera House (1891)
427 Main Street, 72956
250 seats, 2 levels
City of Van Buren
Community theater

California

Columbia
Fallon Theatre (1886)
11175 Washington Street, 95310
250 seats, 2 levels
State of California
Summer playhouse

Monterey
California's First Theater (1846)
Scott and Pacific Streets, 93940
70 seats, 1 level
State of California
Playhouse

Napa
Napa Valley Opera House (1880)
1010 Main Street, 94581
500 seats, 2 levels
Napa Valley Opera House, Inc.
Undergoing restoration
Joseph and Samuel Newson, architects

National City
Granger Hall (1898)
1615 East Fourth Street, 91950
200 seats, 1 level
National City Historical Society
Recital hall
Irving Gill, architect

Nevada City
Nevada Theatre (1865)
401 Broad Street, 95959
368 seats, 2 levels
Nevada Theater Commission
Movies and performances

Pacific Grove
Chautauqua Hall (1889)
162 Sixteenth Street, 93950
350 seats
City of Pacific Grove
Community hall

Sacramento
Eagle Theater (1849; reconstructed 1975)
1025 Front Street, Old Sacramento, 95814
200 seats, 2 levels
California State Parks and Recreation Department
Historical reenactments

San Francisco
Bayview Opera House (1888)
4705 Third Street, 94124
275 seats, 2 levels
City of San Francisco
Community center

Sonora
Sonora Opera Hall (1885)
258 South Washington, 95370
200 seats, 2 levels
City of Sonora
Community center

Winters
Winters Opera House (1875)
13 Main Street, 95694
270 seats
Private partnership
Community hall
D. R. Sackett, builder

Woodland
Woodland Opera House (1896)
Dead Cat Alley, 95695
530 seats, 2 levels
Not-for-profit ownership
Performing arts center

Colorado

Aspen
Wheeler Opera House (1889)
320 East Hyman Avenue, 81611
489 seats, 2 levels
City of Aspen
Performing arts center
Harry W. J. Edbrooke, architect

Boulder
Chautauqua Auditorium (1898)
900 Baseline Road, 80302
1,263 seats
Colorado Chautauqua
    Association
Lectures, films, concerts
    (spring through fall)
Kidder & Rice, architects

Central City
Central City Opera House (1878)
Eureka Street, 80427
753 seats, 2 levels
Central City Opera House
    Association
Summer opera
Robert Roeschlaub, architect

Denver
Elitch Theatre (1891)
West 38 Avenue and Tennyson
    Street, 80221
500 seats, boxes
Elitch Gardens
Closed, pending move in 1997
C. H. Lee & R. Liden,
    architects

Denver
Tivoli Turnhalle (1882)
900 Auraria Parkway, 80204
700 seats, 2 levels
State of Colorado
Meeting facility, special events
Harrold W. Baerresea, architect

Leadville
Tabor Opera House (1879)
308 Harrison Street, 80461
880 seats, 2 levels
Privately owned
Summer performances
    and tours
J. Thomas Roberts,
    architect/builder

Longmont
Dickens Opera House (1881)
302 Main Street, 80501
300 seats
Privately owned
Performances and meetings
William H. Dickens, builder

Ouray
Wright's Opera Hall (1888)
460 Main Street, 81427
200 seats
Privately owned
Summer travelogue screenings
George and Ed White,
    architects

Connecticut

Broad Brook
Broad Brook Opera House
    (1892)
107 Main Street, 06016
200 seats
Privately owned
Plays and meetings
Cook & Hapgood, architects

Chester
Chester Meetinghouse (1795)
Liberty Street and Goose Hill
    Road, 06412
215 seats, 2 levels
Town of Chester
Community uses

Deep River
Deep River Town Hall (1892)
174 Main Street, 06417
350 seats
Town of Deep River
Undergoing renovations

Derby
Sterling Opera House (1889)
Elizabeth Street, 06418
1,200 seats
Sterling Opera Foundation
Undergoing renovations
H. E. Ficken, architect

East Haddam
Goodspeed Opera House (1877)
Goodspeed Landing, 06423
398 seats, 2 levels
Not-for-profit foundation
American musicals
Jebez Comstock, builder

Goshen
Old Town Hall (1895)
2 North Street, 06756
380 seats, 2 levels
Town of Goshen
Meeting hall
Hotchkiss Brothers, architects

Manchester
Cheney Hall (1867)
177 Hartford Road, 06040
332 seats
Town of Manchester
Plays and other performances
Hammat Billings, architect

Norfolk
Norfolk Opera House (1883)
Greenwood Road West, 06058
150 seats
Privately owned
Renovations planned

Stafford
Memorial Hall (1867)
Orcuttville Road, 06075
185 seats
Town of Stafford
Performances

Thomaston
Thomaston Opera House (1884)
158 Main Street, 06787
525 seats, 2 levels
Town of Thomaston
Plays and concerts
Robert W. Hill, architect

Delaware

Wilmington
Grand Opera House (1871)
818 Market Street, 19801
1,110 seats, 2 levels
Not-for-profit corporation
Performing arts center
Thomas Dixson, architect

District of Columbia

Washington, D.C.
Ford's Theatre (1863)
511 10th Street, NW, 20004
700 seats, 2 levels
National Park Service
Museum, performances
James Gifford, architect

Florida

Monticello
Monticello Opera House (1890)
Routes 19 and 90, 32344
363 seats, 2 levels
Not-for-profit corporation
Plays and concerts
W. R. Gunn, architect

Georgia

Brunswick
Ritz Theatre (1899)
1530 Newcastle, 31520
524 seats, 2 levels
City of Brunswick
Multipurpose facility

Columbus
Springer Opera House (1871)
103 Tenth Street, 31902
784 seats, 3 levels
Not-for-profit corporation
Multipurpose facility

Macon
Grand Opera House (1884)
651 Mulberry Street, 31201
1,057 seats, 2 levels
Bibb County
Multipurpose facility
A. Blair and W. R. Gunn,
    architects

Illinois

Chicago
Auditorium Theater (1889)
50 East Congress Parkway,
    60605
4,237 seats, 7 levels
Roosevelt University
Concerts and touring musicals
Dankmar Adler and Louis
    Sullivan, architects

Chicago
Fine Arts Theatres (1898)
410 South Michigan Avenue,
    60605
1,685 seats, now in two theaters
Privately owned
Twin movie theaters
Solon S. Beman, architect

Ellisville
Old Opera House (1891)
Main and Mechanic Streets,
    61431
90 seats
Not-for-profit corporation
Community uses

Elsah
Farley's Music Hall (1885)
41 Mill Street, 62028
70 seats
Historic Elsah Foundation
Undergoing restoration
Frank Farley, builder

Galena
Turner Hall (1874)
115 South Bench Street, 61036
1,000 seats, 2 levels
City of Galena
Community hall

Princeton
Apollo Theater (1883)
455 South Main Street, 61356
720 seats
Kerasotes Theaters
Twin movie theaters

Rushville
Phoenix Opera House (1882)
112 West Lafayette, 62681
200 seats
Not-for-profit corporation
Playhouse; undergoing
    renovations

Sandwich
Sandwich Opera House (1878)
140 East Railroad Street, 60548
310 seats, 2 levels
City of Sandwich
Performances

Woodstock
Woodstock Opera House (1890)
121 Van Buren Street, 60098
429 seats, 2 levels
City of Woodstock
Performances
Smith Hoag, architect

Indiana

Bristol
Bristol Opera House (1897)
210 East Vistula, 46507
192 seats
Not-for-profit corporation
Community theater

Indianapolis
Athenaeum (1898)
401 East Michigan Street, 46204
415 seats, including galleries
The Athenaeum Foundation
    Repertory theater
Vonnegut & Bohn, architects

New Harmony
Thrall's Opera House (1888)
Church Street, 47631
250 seats, 2 levels
State of Indiana
Museum, meeting hall

Remington
Fountain Park Chautauqua
    (1898)
204 North Ohio, 47977
500 seats
Chautauqua Association
Summer entertainment

Valparaiso
Memorial Opera House (1893)
104 Indiana Avenue, 46384
429 seats, 2 levels
Porter County
Plays and community uses

Vevay
Hoosier Theater (1837)
Ferry and Cheapside Streets,
    47043
200 seats
Historic Vevay, Inc.
Movies and performances

Iowa

Dubuque
Grand Opera House (1890)
135 8th Street, 52001
644 seats, 2 levels
Not-for-profit corporation
Plays and concerts

Fonda
Mullen Opera House (1884)
Main Street, 50540
500 seats
Privately owned
Museum

Iowa Falls
Metropolitan Theatre (1899)
Washington Avenue, 50126
522 seats in two theaters
Fridley Theaters
Twin movie theaters

Jefferson
Sierra Theatre (1884)
212 East State Street, 50129
320 seats
Fridley Theaters
Movies

Pella
Pella Opera House (1900)
611 Franklin Street, 50219
328 seats, 2 levels
Pella Opera House Commission
Performing arts center
Stanley de Gooyer, architect

What Cheer
What Cheer Opera House (1893)
Briney and Barnes Streets,
   50268
597 seats, 2 levels
Not-for-profit corporation
Multipurpose facility
J. J. Gordineer, architect

Kansas

Abilene
Plaza Theatre (1879)
402 Northwest 2nd Street, 67410
600 seats
Privately owned
Movies

Junction City
Junction City Opera House
   (1882)
7th and Jefferson Streets, 66441
Planned 500 seats
Opera House Foundation
Undergoing renovation

McPherson
McPherson Opera House (1889)
223 South Main Street, 67460
600 seats, 3 levels planned
McPherson Opera House
   Preservation Company
Tours; undergoing renovation
George Shaffer, architect

Wamego
The Columbian Theatre (1895)
521 Lincoln, 66547
300 seats
Columbian Theatre Foundation
Multipurpose facility
J. C. Rogers, builder

Wilson
Czech Opera House (1901)
415 27th Street, 67490
350 seats, 2 levels
Wilson Czech Opera House
   Corporation
Museum and multipurpose
   facility

Kentucky

Cynthiana
Rohs Opera House (1865)
39 Pike Street, 41031
420 seats since 1941 addition
Privately owned
Upstairs not in use; movies
   shown in the new section

Lexington
Lexington Opera House (1887)
145 North Broadway, 40507
1,040 seats, 3 levels
Lexington Center Corporation
Performing arts center
H. L. Rowe, architect/builder

Maysville
Washington Opera House (1898)
116 West 2nd Street, 41056
600 seats, 3 levels
Maysville Players
Community theater
I. M. Lane & J. D. Easton,
   builders

Maine

Belfast
Belfast Opera House (1866)
59 Church Street, 04915
500 seats
Privately owned
Community uses; now closed

Biddeford
City Theater (1896)
205 Main Street, 04005
552 seats, 2 levels
City of Biddeford
Plays and community uses

Camden
Camden Opera House (1894)
29 Elm Street, 04843
500 seats, 2 levels
City of Camden
Plays and community uses

Damariscotta
Lincoln Theater (1875)
Elm Street, 04543
400 seats
Privately owned
Movies

Gardiner
Johnson Hall Opera House
   (1864)
280 Water Street, 04345
375 seats
Johnson Hall, Inc.
Undergoing renovations,
   open for tours
Ben Johnson, builder

Monmouth
Cumston Hall (1900)
796 Main Street, 04259
307 seats, 2 levels
Town of Monmouth
Summer Shakespeare plays and
   community uses
Harry H. Cochrane, architect
   and builder

Ocean Park
The Temple (1881)
Temple Avenue, 04063
900 seats
Ocean Park Association
Summer camp meetings,
   concerts, movies
Dow and Wheeler, architects

Rockport
Rockport Opera House (1891)
Central Street, 04856
400 seats, 2 levels
Town of Rockport
Multipurpose facility

Saco
Saco City Hall (1856)
300 Main Street, 04072
177 seats, 2 levels
City of Saco
Community uses
Thomas Hill, architect

Maryland

Baltimore
Lyric Opera House (1894)
1404 Maryland Avenue, 21201
2,564 seats, 2 levels
Lyric Foundation
Plays and concerts
T. Henry Randall, architect

Massachusetts

Barre
Town Hall Auditorium (1814)
2 Exchange Street, 01005
200 seats
Town of Barre
Community uses

Boston
Colonial Theatre (1900)
106 Boylston Street, 02116
1,650 seats, 3 levels
Boylston Street Theatre
    Corporation
Touring theatre productions
Clarence Blackall, architect

Boston
Cyclorama (1884)
539 Tremont Street, 02116
876 seats
City of Boston
Performances
Charles Cummings and Willard
    Sears, architects

Boston
State Theatre (1879)
619 Washington Street, 02109
1,147 seats, 3 levels
Privately owned
Adult movies

Boston
Steinert Hall (1896)
162 Boylston Street, 02116
150 seats
Privately owned
Recording studio
Winslow & Wetherell,
    architects

Boston
Symphony Hall (1900)
301 Massachusetts Avenue,
    02199
2,625 seats, 3 levels
Boston Music Hall Corporation
Concert hall
McKim, Mead & White,
    architects

Brewster
Old Town Hall (1881)
Route 6A, 02631
200 seats
Town of Brewster
Community uses
Walter G. Winslow, architect

Brimfield
Brimfield Town Hall (1879)
Main Street, 01010
200 seats
Town of Brimfield
Community uses
E. C. Gardner, architect

Cambridge
Brattle Theatre (1890)
40 Brattle Street, 02138
250 seats, 2 levels
Brattle Square Associates
Movies

Cambridge
Hasty Pudding Theatre (1888)
12 Holyoke Street, 02138
353 seats
Hasty Pudding Club Institution
Performance uses above
    eating club
Peabody & Stearns, architects

Cohasset
Town Hall (1857)
41 Highland Avenue, 02025
250 seats
Town of Cohasset
Community uses

Hingham
Loring Hall (1852)
65 Main Street, 02043
325 seats
Privately owned
Movies
Ammi B. Young, architect

Hyde Park
French's Opera House (1868)
45 Fairmont Avenue, 02136
184 seats
Fairmont Realty Trust
Dinner theater

Marion
Music Hall (1892)
164 Front Street, 02738
140 seats
Town of Marion
Community uses

Methuen
Memorial Music Hall (1899)
192 Broadway, 01844
360 seats, 2 levels
Methuen Memorial Music
    Hall, Inc.
Concert hall
Henry Vaughan, architect

Nantucket
Dreamland (1840)
17 South Water Street, 02554
550 seats
Privately owned
Movies

New Salem
1794 Meeting House (1794)
26 South Main Street, 01355
250 seats
Town of New Salem
Community uses

Northampton
Academy of Music (1891)
274 Main Street, 01060
800 seats, 2 levels
Town of Northampton
Movies and performance uses
William Brocklesby, architect

Provincetown
Provincetown Town Hall (1886)
250 Commercial Street, 02657
708 seats, 2 levels
Town of Provincetown
Community uses
John A. Fox, architect

Shelburne Falls
Memorial Hall (1897)
51 Bridge Street, 01370
425 seats
Town of Shelburne Falls
Community uses, film series

Sherborn
Sherborn Town House (1858)
3 Sanger Street, 01770
225 seats
Community Center Foundation
Community uses

Siasconset
Siasconset Casino (1900)
10 New Street, 02564
350 seats
Siasconset Casino Association
Summer community uses
John Collins, architect

Stockbridge
Berkshire Theater (1888;
    moved 1928)
83 East Main Street, 01262
400 seats, 2 levels
Berkshire Theater Festival, Inc.
Summer playhouse
McKim, Mead & White,
    architects

Taunton
Star Theatre (1875)
4 Court Street, 02780
500 seats, 2 levels
Privately owned
Renovations planned

Uxbridge
Uxbridge Town Hall (1878)
21 South Main Street, 01569
300 seats, 2 levels
Town of Uxbridge
Community uses
Amos P. Cutting, architect

Wendell
Wendell Town Hall (1845)
6 Center Street, 01379
175 seats
Town of Wendell
Community uses

Winchendon
Winchendon Town Hall (1847)
109 Front Street, 01475
250 seats, 2 levels
Town of Winchendon
Veterans center, community
    uses

Worcester
Art Theater (Lothrop's Opera
    House, 1891)
17 Pleasant Street, 001068
250 seats
Privately owned
Adult movies

Worcester
Mechanics Hall (1857)
321 Main Street, 01608
1,600 seats, 2 levels
Worcester County Mechanics
    Association
Meetings and performance uses
Elbridge Boyden, architect

Worthington
Sevenars Hall (1825)
South Ireland Street, 01098
330 seats
Privately owned
Concert hall; summer music
    festival

Michigan

Adrian
Croswell Opera House (1866)
129 East Maumee Street, 49221
659 seats, 2 levels
Croswell Opera House and Fine
    Arts Association
Performing arts center

Calumet
Calumet Theater (1900)
340 6th Street, 49913
711 seats, 2 levels
Town of Calumet
Performing arts center
Charles K. Shand, architect

Cheboygan
Cheboygan Opera House (1877)
403 North Huron Street, 49721
582 seats, 2 levels
City of Cheboygan
Performing arts center

Coldwater
Tibbit's Opera House (1882)
14 South Hanchett, 49036
550 seats, 2 levels
Tibbit's Opera Foundation and
    Arts Council Inc.
Performing arts center
Mortimer Smith, architect

Grand Ledge
Grand Ledge Opera House
    (1884)
121 South Bridge Street, 48837
300 seats, 2 levels
Opera House Authority
Community hall

Stockbridge
Stockbridge Town Hall (1893)
100 South Clinton Street, 49285
300 seats, 2 levels
Town of Stockbridge
    Community hall
Elijah E. Myers, architect

Traverse City
City Opera House (1892)
118 East Front Street, 49684
220 seats, 2 levels
City of Traverse City
Performances
E. R. Prall, architect

Vermontville
Vermontville Opera House
    (1898)
South Main Street, 49096
165 seats, 2 levels
Township of Vermontville
Community uses

Minnesota

Cokato
Temperance Hall (1896)
County Road 3, 55321
100 seats
Finnish Historical Society
Annual tour

Lake Benton
Lake Benton Opera House
    (1896)
P.O. Box 1, 56149
275 seats, 2 levels
Lake Benton Opera House, Inc.
Community hall

St. Paul
CSPS (Sokol) Hall (1887)
383 Michigan Street, 55102
160 seats
Sokol Organization
Community center
Emil W. Ulrici, architect

Mississippi

Meridian
Grand Opera House (1890)
2208 Fifth Street, 39301
1,500 seats, 3 levels
Grand Opera House of
    Mississippi, Inc.
Tours and performances
J. B. McElfatrick, architect

Missouri

Boonville
Thespian Hall (1857)
522 Main Street, 65233
638 seats, 2 levels
Friends of Historic Boonville
Performing arts center
John L. Howard, architect

Greenfield
Greenfield Opera House (1888)
Town Square, 65661
250 seats
Opera House Corporation
Summer playhouse

Kansas City
Folly Theater (1900)
300 West Twelfth Street, 64105
1,175 seats, 2 levels
Performing Arts Foundation
Performing arts center
Louis Curtiss, architect

Montana

Phillipsburg
McDonald Opera House (1891)
59858
250 seats
Privately owned
Movies

Nebraska

David City
Thorpe Opera House (1889)
461½ D Street, 68632
250 seats
Privately owned
Community hall

Fremont
Fremont Opera House (1888)
541 North Broad Street, 68025
1,175 seats
Not-for-profit corporation
Community uses downstairs;
    awaiting renovation

Red Cloud
Red Cloud Opera House (1885)
326 North Webster, 68970
200 seats
Willa Cather Pioneer Memorial
Scheduled to reopen for
    community uses following
    renovations, 1998

Table Rock
Table Rock Opera House (1893)
Main Street, 68447
100 seats
Table Rock Historical
    Association
Museum

Nevada

Eureka
Eureka Opera House (1880)
1021 Main Street, 89316
314 seats, 2 levels
Town of Eureka
Meeting space and
    performances

Pioche
Thompson's Opera House (1873)
North Main Street, 89043
No seats at present
Lincoln County
Undergoing renovation

Virginia City
Piper's Opera House (1885)
B and Union Streets, 89440
900 seats, and balcony pews
State of Nevada
Summer tours and some
    performances

New Hampshire

Claremont
Claremont Opera House (1897)
City Hall, Tremont Square,
    03743
775 seats, 2 levels
Claremont Opera House, Inc.
Performing arts center
Charles Rich, architect

Franklin
Franklin Opera House (1892)
316 Central Street, 03235
400 seats, 2 levels
City of Franklin
Council chambers; renovation
    planned
H. H. Richardson, architect

Littleton
Littleton Opera House (1895)
1 Union Street, 03561
400 seats, 2 levels
Town of Littleton
Performance and community
    uses
Fred T. Austin, architect

Newport
Newport Opera House (1886)
20 Main Street, 03773
650 seats, 2 levels
Town of Newport
Multipurpose facility
F. N. Footman, architect

Plainfield
Plainfield Town Hall (1798)
Route 12A, 03781
160 seats
Town of Plainfield
Multipurpose facility

Portsmouth
Music Hall (1878)
28 Chestnut Street, 03801
900 seats, 2 levels
Friends of the Music Hall
Movies and performances
William A. Ashe, architect

Washington
Washington Town Hall (1789)
Town Hall, 03280
200 seats
Town of Washington
Community hall

New Jersey

Ocean Grove
Great Auditorium (1894)
Pilgrim Pathway, 07756
6,500 seats, 2 levels
Ocean Grove Camp Meeting
    Association
Chautauqua events
Fred T. Camp, architect

New Mexico

Socorro
Garcia Opera House (1886)
100 Abeyta Street, 87801
308 seats
Privately owned
Multipurpose facility

New York

Brooklyn
Grand Prospect Hall (1901)
263 Prospect Avenue, 11215
2,000 seats
Privately owned
Multipurpose facility
Ulrich J. Huberty, architect

Cambridge
Hubbard Hall (1878)
25 East Main Street, 12816
190 seats
Hubbard Hall Projects, Inc.
Community uses
Marcus Cummings, architect

Chautauqua
Chautauqua Amphitheater
    (1893)
Clark Avenue, 14722
5,500 seats
Chautauqua Institution
Chautauqua programs and
    concerts
Ellis G. Hall, architect

Cohoes
Cohoes Music Hall (1874)
58 Remsen Street, 12047
300 seats, 2 levels
City of Cohoes
Visitors center and
    performances
Charles Nichols &
    J. B. Halcott, architects

Earlville
Earlville Opera House (1892)
P.O. Box 111, 13332
300 seats, 2 levels
Earlville Opera House
    Association
Plays and community uses

Fredonia
Fredonia Opera House (1891)
Town Square, 14063
430 seats, 2 levels
Village of Fredonia
Community uses
Enoch Curtis, architect

Geneva
Smith Opera House (1894)
82 Seneca Street, 14456
1,365 seats, 2 levels
Finger Lakes Regional Arts
    Council
Movies and performances
Pierce-Bickford, architects

Hudson
Hudson Opera House (1855)
327 Warren Street, 12534
400 seats
Hudson Opera House Inc.
Undergoing renovation
Peter Avery, architect

Lancaster
Lancaster Opera House (1897)
21 Central Avenue, 14086
487 seats, 2 levels
Town of Lancaster
Performing arts center
George J. Metzger, architect

New York City
Carnegie Hall (1891)
881 7th Avenue, 10019
3,072 seats, 5 levels
City of New York
Concert hall
William Burnett Tuthill,
    architect

New York City
New Victory Theater (1900)
207 West 42nd Street, 10036
500 seats
New York State
Playhouse
Albert E. Westover, architect

New York City
Webster Hall (1886)
119–123 East Eleventh Street,
    10003
3,000 seats, 5 levels
Private owner
Popular concerts
Charles Rentz, architect

Poughkeepsie
Bardavon Opera House (1869)
35 Market Street, 12601
994 seats, 2 levels
Bardavon 1869 Opera House Inc.
Performing arts center
James Post, architect

Poughkeepsie
Vassar Brothers Institute (1883)
12 Vassar Street, 12601
190 seats
Civic Properties Inc.
Lectures, performances,
    and movies
J. A. Woods, architect

Pultneyville
Gates Hall (1826)
Westlake Road, 14538
110 seats
Landmarks Society
Community uses

Rhinebeck
Starr Institute (1862)
26 Montgomery Street, 12571
160 seats
Upstate Films
Movies

Riverhead
Music Hall (1881)
18 Peconic Avenue, 11901
350 seats, 3 levels
Council for the Vail-Leavitt
    Music Hall, Inc.
Movies

Round Lake
Round Lake Auditorium (1868)
Round Lake, 12151
450 seats
Village of Round Lake
Chautauqua programs

Tarrytown
Music Hall (1885)
13 Main Street, 10591
840 seats, 2 levels
Friends of the Mozartina
    Conservatory
Performing arts and movies
Philip Edmunds, architect

Troy
Troy Savings Bank Music Hall
    (1875)
32 Second Street, 12180
1,255 seats, 3 levels
Troy Savings Bank
Concert hall and recording
    studio
George B. Post, architect

North Carolina

Kernersville
Korner's Folly (1880)
South Main Street, 27284
60 seats
Privately owned
Museum; occasional
    performances
Jule Korner, builder

Wilmington
Thalian Hall (1858)
310 Chestnut Street, 28402
750 seats, 3 levels
City of Wilmington
Performing arts center
John Montague Trimble,
    architect

North Dakota

Lisbon
Lisbon Opera House (1889)
413 Main Street, 58054
300 seats, 2 levels
Lisbon Opera House
    Foundation
Periodic exhibitions

Ohio

Bellville
Bellville Opera House (1877)
89 Highland Avenue, 44813
150 seats
Village of Bellville
Community uses

Cedarville
Cedarville Opera House (1888)
P.O. Box 685, 45314
640 seats
Cedarville Opera House Society
Community programs

Chillicothe
Majestic Theatre (1853)
45 East Second Street, 45601
535 seats, 2 levels
Majestic Theatre, Inc.
Movies and performances
John F. Cook, architect

Cincinnati
Music Hall (1878)
1243 Elm Street, 45210
3,417 seats, 3 levels
City of Cincinnati
Concert hall and other
    performances
Hannaford & Proctor,
    architects

Columbus
Southern Theatre (1896)
21 East Main Street, 43215
3 levels, under construction
Columbus Association for the
    Performing Arts
To reopen May 1998
Dauben, Krumm & Riebel,
    architects

Cleveland
Bohemian Hall (1897)
4939 Broadway, 44127
500 seats
Sokol Greater Cleveland
Community uses

Dayton
Victoria Theatre (1866)
138 North Main Street, 45402
1,139 seats
Victoria Theatre Association
Performing arts center

Gallipolis
Ariel Theatre (1895)
426 Second Street, 45631
465 seats, 2 levels
Gallipolis Masonic Lodge
Multipurpose facility
J. W. Yost, architect

Genoa
Genoa Opera House (1885)
6th and Main Streets, 43430
239 seats
Village of Genoa
Community uses

Hayesville
Hayesville Opera House (1886)
7 East Main Street, 44838
250 seats
Town of Hayesville
Tours
Sam Craig, architect

Lakeside
South Auditorium (1884)
Central and 6th Streets, 43440
700 seats
Lakeside Association
Chautauqua programs

McConnelsville
McConnelsville Opera House
    (1892)
15 West Main Street, 43756
563 seats, 2 levels
Town of McConnelsville and
    private owners
Movies and plays
H. C. Lindsay, architect

Middletown
Sorg Opera House (1891)
57 South Main Street, 45044
765 seats, 2 levels
Privately owned
Performances
Samuel Hannaford, architect

Mount Vernon
Woodward Opera House (1853)
103 South Main Street, 43050
300 seats, 2 levels
Privately owned
Tours (August and November)

Nelsonville
Stuart's Opera House (1879)
Public Square, 45764
600 seats, 2 levels
Hocking Valley Museum of
    Theatrical History
Undergoing renovation
W. H. Voorhees, architect

Put-in-Bay
Put-in-Bay Town Hall (1887)
Catawba Avenue, 43456
Removable seats
Town of Put-in-Bay
Community uses
George Cascoyne, architect

Rising Sun
Rising Sun Opera House (1901)
420 Main Street, 43457
300 seats, 2 levels
Village of Rising Sun
Community uses
Allie E. Johnson, architect

Toledo
Valentine Theater (1895)
Adams and St. Clair Streets,
   43604
1,904 seats, 2 levels
City of Toledo
Restoration planned

Oregon

Salem
Grand Theater (1900)
191 High Street, 97301
400 seats, 2 levels
Odd Fellows Lodge
Now closed

Pennsylvania

Allentown
Symphony Hall (1899)
23 North 6th Street, 18101
1,549 seats, 3 levels
Allentown Symphony
   Association
Concerts and plays
J. B. McElfatrick, architect

Brookville
Marlin's Opera House (1886)
225–237 Main Street, 15825
900 seats, 3 levels
Privately owned
Tours (December and June)

Jim Thorpe
Mauch Chunk Opera House
   (1881)
14 West Broadway, 18229
275 seats, 2 levels
Mauch Chunk Historical Society
Multipurpose facility
Balderson & Hutton, architects

Lancaster
Fulton Opera House (1852)
12 North Prince Street, 17603
684 seats, 3 levels
Fulton Opera House Foundation
Performing arts center
Samuel Sloane, architect

Meadville
Academy Theatre (1885)
275 Chestnut Street, 16335
600 seats
Academy Theatre Foundation
Performances
J. M. Woods, architect

Mount Gretna
Mount Gretna Playhouse (1892)
Pennsylvania Avenue, 17064
650 seats
Mount Gretna Chautauqua
   Association
Plays and concerts
John Cilley, architect

Munhall
Carnegie Library of Homestead
   Music Hall (1898)
510 10th Avenue, 15120
1,033 seats, 2 levels
Not-for-profit foundation
Concert hall and community
   uses
Longfellow, Alden & Harlow,
   architects

Oakland
Carnegie Music Hall (1895)
4400 Forbes Avenue, 15213
1,950 seats
Not-for-profit foundation
Concerts and lectures
Longfellow, Alden & Harlow,
   architects

Philadelphia
Academy of Music (1857)
Broad and Locust Streets, 19102
2,929 seats, 3 levels
Philadelphia Orchestra
   Association
Concerts and performances
Napoleon Le Brun &
   Gustavus Runge, architects

Philadelphia
Trocadero (1870)
1003 Arch Street
1,000 possible seats
Private
Concert venue
Edwin F. Durang and George
   Plowman, architects

Philadelphia
Walnut Street Theatre (1809)
825 Walnut Street, 19107
1,052 seats, 2 levels
Walnut Street Theatre Inc.
Theatre productions
John Haviland, architect

Pittsburgh
Carnegie Free Library and
   Hazlett Theater (1888)
Allegheny Square, 15212
457 seats
City of Pittsburgh
Theatre productions
Smithmeyer & Pelz, architects

Pittsburgh
Plaza Theatre (1900)
4765 Liberty Avenue, 15212
336 seats, 2 theaters
Catholic Church
Twin movie theater

Towanda
Keystone Theatre (1886)
601 Main Street, 18848
550 seats, 2 levels
Bradford County Regional Arts
   Council
Multipurpose facility

Warren
Library Theatre (1883)
302 3rd Avenue West, 16365
995 seats, 2 levels
Charitable trust and Town of
   Warren
Performing arts center
D. K. Dean, architect

Rhode Island

Newport
Casino Theatre (1880)
Bellevue Avenue, 02840
410 seats, 2 levels
The Newport Casino
Vacant; tours by appointment
McKim, Mead & White,
    architects

South Carolina

Bishopville
Bishopville Opera House (1890)
109 North Main Street, 29010
300 seats
Lee County Arts Council
Community uses

Charleston
Dock Street Theatre (1736;
    reconstructed 1937)
Church Street, 29403
463 seats
City of Charleston
Performing arts center

Charleston
McCrady's Long Room (1778)
153 East Bay Street, 29401
Dining room seating
Long Room Restaurant
Stage area as needed
Edward McCrady, builder

Marion
Marion Opera House (1892)
109 West Godbolt Street, 29571
525 seats
City of Marion
Community uses

Newberry
Newberry Opera House (1882)
1201 McKibben Street, 29108
400 seats, 2 levels
City of Newberry
Undergoing renovation
G. L. Norman, architect

Sumter
Sumter Opera House (1893)
21 North Main, 29150
610 seats, 2 levels
City of Sumter
Performing arts center
J. C. Turner, architect

Tennessee

Nashville
Ryman Auditorium (1892)
116 Fifth Avenue North, 37219
2,332 seats in pews
Gaylord Entertainment
    Company
Visitor center and performances
A.T. Thompson, architect

Texas

Bastrop
Bastrop Opera House (1890)
711 Spring Street, 78602
250 seats
Bastrop Opera House
    Association
Community uses
David Green and P. O. Elzner,
    architects

Columbus
Stafford Opera House (1886)
425 Spring Street, 78934
600 seats, 2 levels
Magnolia Homes Tours Inc.
Community uses
Nicholas J. Clayton, architect

Galveston
Grand 1894 Opera House (1895)
2020 Postoffice Street, 77550
1,040 seats, 3 levels
1894 Inc.
Performing arts center
Frank Cox, architect

Granbury
Granbury Opera House (1886)
116 West Pearl Street, 76048
303 seats, 2 levels
Granbury Opera House
Association
Playhouse

Henderson
Henderson Opera House (1865)
122 East Main Street, 75652
180 seats
Henderson Civic Theatre Inc.
Playhouse

Uvalde
Grand Opera House (1891)
104 West North Street, 78801
370 seats, 2 levels
City of Uvalde
Community uses
B. F. Trister, Jr., architect

Utah

St. George
St. George Social Hall (1864)
200 North Main Street, 84770
200 seats
City of St. George
Community uses

Vermont

Barre
Barre Opera House (1899)
North Main and Prospect
    Streets, 05641
650 seats, 2 levels
City of Barre
Performing arts center
George G. Adams, architect

Bethel
Bethel Town Hall (1893)
Main Street, 05032
100 seats, 2 levels
Town of Bethel
Rental for performance uses
George Guernsey, architect

Bristol
Holley Hall (1890)
West Street, 05443
350 seats, 2 levels
Town of Bristol
Community uses

Derby Line, Vt., and Rock
    Island, Quebec
Haskell Free Library and Opera
    House (1904)
Main Street, 05830
648 seats, 2 levels
North County Concert
    Association
Performing arts center
James Ball, architect

Enosburgh Falls
Enosburgh Opera House (1892)
Depot Street, 05450
200 seats
Town of Enosburgh
Community uses

Hardwick
Hardwick Town House (1850)
25 Church Street, 05843
500 seats, 2 levels
Town of Hardwick
Community uses

Pawlet
Pawlet Town Hall (1861)
School Street, 05761
150 seats
Town of Pawlet
Community uses

South Londonderry
Londonderry Town Hall (1860)
Middletown Road, 05155
175 seats, 2 levels
Town of South Londonderry
Community uses

Vergennes
Vergennes Opera House (1897)
Main Street, 05491
420 seats
Town of Vergennes
Undergoing renovation;
    opening scheduled 1997
Chappel & Smith, architects

White River Junction
Briggs Opera House (1890)
12 South Main Street, 05001
245 seats
Privately owned
Playhouse

Woodstock
Town Hall Theatre (1900)
29 The Green, 05091
450 seats, 2 levels
Town of Woodstock
Community theatre

Virginia

Abingdon
Barter Theatre (1833)
133 West Main Street, 24212
402 seats, 2 levels
Town of Abingdon
Playhouse

Pocahontas
Pocahontas Opera House (1895)
Box 127, 24635
200 seats
Town of Pocahontas
Dinner theatre

Wisconsin

Argyle
Star Theatre (1878)
200 South State Street, 53504
100 of 400 seats in use
Privately owned
Summer plays
Alanson Partridge, architect

Columbus
City Hall Auditorium (1892)
105 North Dickason Boulevard,
    53925
540 seats, 2 levels
Town of Columbus
Tours; undergoing renovation
T. D. Allen, architect

Fifield
Old Town Hall Museum (1894)
7213 West Pine Street, 54524
No seats at present
Price County
Museum

Hazel Green
Hazel Green Opera House (1891)
21st and Main Streets, 53811
90 seats, 2 levels
Privately owned
For sale

Menomonie
Mabel Tainter Memorial Theater
    (1890)
205 Main Street, 54751
313 seats, 2 levels
City of Menomonie
Multipurpose facility
Harvey Ellis, architect

Milwaukee
Pabst Theater (1895)
114 East Wells, 53202
1,388 seats, 3 levels
City of Milwaukee
Performing arts center
Otto Strack, architect

Oshkosh
Grand Opera House (1883)
100 High Street, 54902
704 seats, 2 levels
City of Oshkosh
Performing arts center
William Walters, architect

Stoughton
City Hall Theater (1901)
381 East Main Street, 53589
650 seats, 2 levels
City of Stoughton
Plays and community uses
F. H. Kemp, architect

Wyoming

Cheyenne
Atlas Theater (1887)
213 West 16th Street, 82003
256 seats
Cheyenne Little Theater Players
Plays and performances
William Dubois, architect

Chronological List of Theaters

Arranged alphabetically
under year of opening

1736

Dock Street Theatre,
　Charleston, S.C.
　(reconstructed 1937)

1778

McCrady's Long Room,
　Charleston, S.C.

1789

Town Hall, Washington, N.H.

1794

Meeting House,
　New Salem, Mass.

1795

Chester Meetinghouse,
　Chester, Conn.

1798

Plainfield Town Hall,
　Plainfield, N.H.

1809

Walnut Street Theatre,
　Philadelphia, Pa.

1814

Barre Town Hall, Barre, Mass.

1825

Sevenars Hall,
　Worthington, Mass.

1826

Gates Hall, Pultneyville, N.Y.

1833

Barter Theatre, Abingdon, Va.

1837

Hoosier Theater, Vevay, Ind.

1840

Dreamland, Nantucket, Mass.

1845

Wendell Town Hall,
　Wendell, Mass.

1846

California's First Theater,
　Monterey, Calif.

1847

Winchendon Town Hall,
　Winchendon, Mass.

1849

Eagle Theater, Sacramento,
　Calif. (reconstructed 1975)

1850

Hardwick Town House,
　Hardwick, Vt.

1852

Fulton Opera House,
　Lancaster, Pa.
Loring Hall, Hingham, Mass.

1853

Majestic Theatre,
　Chillicothe, Ohio
Woodward Opera House,
　Mount Vernon, Ohio

1855

Hudson Opera House,
　Hudson, N.Y.

1856

Saco City Hall, Saco, Maine

1857

Academy of Music,
　Philadelphia, Pa.
Mechanics Hall, Worcester, Mass.
Thespian Hall, Boonville, Mo.
Town Hall, Cohasset, Mass.

1858

Sherborn Town House,
　Sherborn, Mass.
Thalian Hall, Wilmington, N.C.

1860

Londonderry Town Hall, South
　Londonderry, Vt.

1861

Pawlet Town Hall, Pawlet, Vt.

1862

Starr Institute, Rhinebeck, N.Y.

1863

Ford's Theatre, Washington, D.C.

1864

Johnson Hall Opera House,
　Gardiner, Maine
St. George Social Hall,
　St. George, Utah

1865

Henderson Opera House,
　Henderson, Tex.
Nevada Theatre,
　Nevada City, Calif.
Rohs Opera House,
　Cynthiana, Ky.

The Barter Theater (1833) in Abingdon, Virginia, was operated on the barter system for a short while, after its conversion to a theater in 1933.

1866

Belfast Opera House,
    Belfast, Maine
Croswell Opera House,
    Adrian, Mich.
Victoria Theatre, Dayton, Ohio

1867

Cheney Hall, Manchester, Conn.
Memorial Hall, Stafford, Conn.

1868

French's Opera House,
    Hyde Park, Mass.
Round Lake Auditorium,
    Round Lake, N.Y.

1869

Bardavon Opera House,
    Poughkeepsie, N.Y.

1870

Trocadero, Philadelphia, Pa.

1871

Grand Opera House,
    Wilmington, Del.
Springer Opera House,
    Columbus, Ga.

1873

Thompson's Opera House,
    Pioche, Nev.

1874

Cohoes Music Hall,
    Cohoes, N.Y.
Turner Hall, Galena, Ill.

1875

Lincoln Theater,
    Damariscotta, Maine
Star Theatre, Taunton, Mass.
Troy Savings Bank Music Hall,
    Troy, N.Y.
Winters Opera House,
    Winters, Calif.

1877

Bellville Opera House,
    Bellville, Ohio
Cheboygan Opera House,
    Cheboygan, Mich.
Goodspeed Opera House,
    East Haddam, Conn.

1878

Central City Opera House,
    Central City, Colo.
Hubbard Hall, Cambridge, N.Y.
Music Hall, Cincinnati, Ohio
Music Hall, Portsmouth, N.H.
Sandwich Opera House,
    Sandwich, Ill.
Star Theatre, Argyle, Wis.
Uxbridge Town Hall,
    Uxbridge, Mass.

1879

Brimfield Town Hall,
    Brimfield, Mass.
Plaza Theatre, Abilene, Kans.
State Theatre, Boston, Mass.
Stuart's Opera House,
    Nelsonville, Ohio
Tabor Opera House,
    Leadville, Colo.

1880

Casino Theater, Newport, R.I.
Eureka Opera House,
    Eureka, Nev.
Korner's Folly, Kernersville, N.C.
Napa Valley Opera House,
    Napa, Calif.

1881

Bird Cage Theatre,
    Tombstone, Ariz.
Dickens Opera House,
    Longmont, Colo.
Mauch Chunk Opera House,
    Jim Thorpe, Pa.
Music Hall, Riverhead, N.Y.
Old Town Hall, Brewster, Mass.
Schieffelin Hall,
    Tombstone, Ariz.
The Temple, Ocean Park, Maine

1882

Junction City Opera House,
 Junction City, Kans.
Newberry Opera House,
 Newberry, S.C.
Phoenix Opera House,
 Rushville, Ill.
Tibbit's Opera House,
 Coldwater, Mich.
Tivoli Turnhalle, Denver, Colo.

1883

Apollo Theater, Princeton, Ill.
Grand Opera House,
 Oshkosh, Wis.
Library Theatre, Warren, Pa.
Norfolk Opera House,
 Norfolk, Conn.
Vassar Brothers Institute,
 Poughkeepsie, N.Y.

1884

Cyclorama, Boston, Mass.
Grand Ledge Opera House,
 Grand Ledge, Mich.
Grand Opera House, Macon, Ga.
Mullen Opera House,
 Fonda, Iowa
Sierra Theatre, Jefferson, Iowa
South Auditorium,
 Lakeside, Ohio
Thomaston Opera House,
 Thomaston, Conn.

1885

Academy Theatre,
 Meadville, Pa.
Farley's Music Hall, Elsah, Ill.
Genoa Opera House,
 Genoa, Ohio
Music Hall, Tarrytown, N.Y.
Piper's Opera House,
 Virginia City, Nev.
Red Cloud Opera House,
 Red Cloud, Neb.
Sonora Opera Hall,
 Sonora, Calif.

1886

Fallon Theatre, Columbia, Calif.
Garcia Opera House,
 Socorro, N.M.
Granbury Opera House,
 Granbury, Tex.
Hayesville Opera House,
 Hayesville, Ohio
Keystone Theatre, Towanda, Pa.
Marlin's Opera House,
 Brookville, Pa.
Newport Opera House,
 Newport, N.H.
Provincetown Town Hall,
 Provincetown, Mass.
Stafford Opera House,
 Columbus, Tex.
Webster Hall, New York, N.Y.

1887

Atlas Theater,
 Cheyenne, Wyo.
CSPS (Sokol) Hall,
 St. Paul, Minn.
Lexington Opera House,
 Lexington, Ky.
Put-in-Bay Town Hall,
 Put-in-Bay, Ohio

1888

Bayview Opera House,
 San Francisco, Calif.
Berkshire Theater,
 Stockbridge, Mass.
Carnegie Free Library
 and Hazlett Theater,
 Pittsburgh, Pa.
Cedarville Opera House,
 Cedarville, Ohio
Fremont Opera House,
 Fremont, Neb.
Greenfield Opera House,
 Greenfield, Mo.
Hasty Pudding Theatre,
 Cambridge, Mass.
Thrall's Opera House,
 New Harmony, Ind.
Wright's Opera Hall,
 Ouray, Colo.

1889

Auditorium Theater,
 Chicago, Ill.
Chautauqua Hall,
 Pacific Grove, Calif.
Lisbon Opera House,
 Lisbon, N.D.
McPherson Opera House,
 McPherson, Kans.
Sterling Opera House,
 Derby, Conn.
Thorpe Opera House,
 David City, Neb.
Thrall's Opera House,
 New Harmony, Ind.
Wheeler Opera House,
 Aspen, Colo.

1890

Bastrop Opera House,
 Bastrop, Tex.
Bishopville Opera House,
 Bishopville, S.C.
Brattle Theatre,
 Cambridge, Mass.
Briggs Opera House,
 White River Junction, Vt.
Fort Payne Opera House,
 Fort Payne, Ala.
Grand Opera House,
 Dubuque, Iowa
Grand Opera House,
 Meridian, Miss.
Holley Hall, Bristol, Vt.
Mabel Tainter Memorial
 Theater, Menomonie, Wis.
Monticello Opera House,
 Monticello, Fla.
Woodstock Opera House,
 Woodstock, Ill.

1891

Academy of Music,
 Northampton, Mass.
Art Theater, Worcester, Mass.
Carnegie Hall, New York, N.Y.
Elitch Theatre, Denver, Colo.
Fredonia Opera House,
 Fredonia, N.Y.
Grand Opera House,
 Uvalde, Tex.
Hazel Green Opera House,
 Hazel Green, Wis.
King Opera House,
 Van Buren, Ark.
McDonald Opera House,
 Phillipsburg, Mont.
Old Opera House, Ellisville, Ill.
Rockport Opera House,
 Rockport, Maine
Sorg Opera House,
 Middletown, Ohio

1892

Broad Brook Opera House,
  Broad Brook, Conn.
City Hall Auditorium,
  Columbus, Wis.
Deep River Town Hall,
  Deep River, Conn.
Earlville Opera House,
  Earlville, N.Y.
Enosburgh Opera House,
  Enosburgh Falls, Vt.
Franklin Opera House,
  Franklin, N.H.
Marion Opera House,
  Marion, S.C.
McConnelsville Opera House,
  McConnelsville, Ohio
Mount Gretna Playhouse,
  Mount Gretna, Pa.
Music Hall, Marion, Mass.
Ryman Auditorium,
  Nashville, Tenn.
Traverse City Opera House,
  Traverse City, Mich.

1893

Bethel Town Hall, Bethel, Vt.
Chautauqua Amphitheater,
  Chautauqua, N.Y.
Memorial Opera House,
  Valparaiso, Ind.
Stockbridge Town Hall,
  Stockbridge, Mich.
Sumter City Hall Opera House,
  Sumter, S.C.
Table Rock Opera House,
  Table Rock, Neb.
What Cheer Opera House,
  What Cheer, Iowa

1894

Camden Opera House,
  Camden, Maine
Great Auditorium,
  Ocean Grove, N.J.
Lyric Opera House,
  Baltimore, Md.
Old Town Hall Museum,
  Fifield, Wis.
Smith Opera House,
  Geneva, N.Y.

1895

Ariel Theatre,
  Gallipolis, Ohio
Carnegie Music Hall,
  Oakland, Pa.
Columbian Theatre,
  Wamego, Kans.
Grand 1894 Opera House,
  Galveston, Tex.
Littleton Opera House,
  Littleton, N.H.
Old Town Hall, Goshen, Conn.
Pabst Theater, Milwaukee, Wis.
Pocahontas Opera House,
  Pocahontas, Va.
Valentine Theater, Toledo,
  Ohio

1896

City Theater, Biddeford,
  Maine
Lake Benton Opera House,
  Lake Benton, Minn.
Southern Theatre,
  Columbus, Ohio
Steinert Hall, Boston, Mass.
Temperance Hall, Cokato, Minn.
Woodland Opera House,
  Woodland, Calif.

1897

Bohemian Hall, Cleveland, Ohio
Bristol Opera House,
  Bristol, Ind.
Claremont Opera House,
  Claremont, N.H.
Lancaster Opera House,
  Lancaster, N.Y.
Memorial Hall,
  Shelburne Falls, Mass.
Vergennes Opera House,
  Vergennes, Vt.

1898

Athenaeum, Indianapolis, Ind.
Carnegie Library of Homestead
  Music Hall, Munhall, Pa.
Chautauqua Auditorium,
  Boulder, Colo.
Fine Arts Theatres, Chicago, Ill.
Fountain Park Chautauqua,
  Remington, Ind.
Granger Hall, National City,
  Calif.
Vermontville Opera House,
  Vermontville, Mich.
Washington Opera House,
  Maysville, Ky.

1899

Barre Opera House, Barre, Vt.
Memorial Music Hall,
  Methuen, Mass.
Metropolitan Theatre,
  Iowa Falls, Iowa
Ritz Theatre, Brunswick, Ga.
Symphony Hall, Allentown, Pa.

1900

Calumet Theater,
  Calumet, Mich.
Colonial Theatre, Boston, Mass.
Cumston Hall,
  Monmouth, Maine
Folly Theater, Kansas City, Mo.
Grand Theater, Salem, Oreg.
New Victory Theater,
  New York, N.Y.
Pella Opera House, Pella, Iowa
Plaza Theatre, Pittsburgh, Pa.
Siasconset Casino,
  Siasconset, Mass.
Symphony Hall, Boston, Mass.
Town Hall Theatre,
  Woodstock, Vt.

1901

City Hall Theater,
  Stoughton, Wis.
Czech Opera House,
  Wilson, Kans.
Grand Prospect Hall,
  Brooklyn, N.Y.
Rising Sun Opera House,
  Rising Sun, Ohio

1904

Haskell Free Library and Opera
  House, Derby Line, Vt.,
  and Rock Island, Quebec

Bibliography

The Auditorium Theater. Chicago: Auditorium Theater Council, undated pamphlet.

Beasley, Ellen. "The End of the Rainbow." *Historic Preservation*, March–June 1972, 18–23.

Bellman, Willard F. *Lighting the Stage: Art and Practice*. San Francisco: Chandler, 1967.

———. *Scenography and Stage Technology*. New York: Thomas Y. Crowell, 1977.

Brockett, Oscar G. *History of the Theater*. Boston: Allyn & Bacon, 1995.

Burns, Richard, ed. *Chautauqua by the Sea*. Annual program and directory. Ocean Park, Maine: 1993.

Cahn, Julius. *Julius Cahn's Official Theatrical Guide*. New York: Publication Office, Empire Theatre Building, 1899–1914.

Calnek, Anthony. *The Hasty Pudding Theatre*. New York: A.D.C., A.O.M.F., 1986.

Carlson, Marvin. *Palaces of Performance: The Semiotics of Theatre Architecture*. Ithaca, N.Y.: Cornell University Press, 1992.

Central City Opera House. *Central City Opera: Looking Back over Sixty Years 1932–1992*. Central City, Colo.: Central City Opera House, 1992.

Edwards, John C. "A History of Nineteenth Century Theatre Architecture in the United States." Ph.D. diss., Northwestern University, 1963.

Eiland, William U. *Nashville's Mother Church: The History of the Ryman Auditorium*. Old Hickory, Tenn.: Opryland U.S.A., 1992.

Erskine, Margaret A. *Mechanics Hall*. Worcester, Mass.: Bicentennial Commission, 1977.

Floyd, Margaret Henderson. *Architecture after Richardson*. Chicago: University of Chicago Press, 1994.

Folly Theater. *Encore: The Reopening of the Folly Theater*. Kansas City, Mo.: Folly Theater, 1981.

Frick, John W., with Carlton Ward, eds. *Directory of Historic American Theatres*. Westport, Conn.: Greenwood Press, League of Historic American Theatres, 1987.

Furman, Evelyn Livingston. *The Tabor Opera House: A Captivating History*. Aurora, Colo.: National Writers Press, 1972.

Gatz, Gerald. "The Construction of the Claremont Opera House." *Historical New Hampshire* 37, no. 1 (1982).

Glazer, Irvin. *Philadelphia Theaters: A Pictorial Architectural History*. New York: Dover, Athenaeum of Philadelphia, 1994.

Glenn, George D., with Richard L. Poole. *The Opera House of Iowa*. Ames, Iowa: University of Iowa Press, 1993.

Gurtler, Jack, with Corinne Hunt. *The Elitch Garden Story*. Boulder, Colo.: Rocky Mountain Writers Guild, 1982.

Hall, Ben. *The Best Remaining Seats*. New York: Bramhall, 1961.

Heller, Mary Wheeler. *A Casino Album*. Siasconset, Mass.: 1974.

Hemsley, Gilbert V., Jr. "A History of Stage Lighting in America 1879–1917." Master's thesis, Yale University, 1960.

Henderson, Mary. *The City and the Theater*. Clifton, N.J.: James T. White & Co., 1973.

Historic Preservation. Magazine of the National Trust for Historic Preservation, Washington, D.C., 1949–96.

Hoffmeier, Ginger. *The First 100 Years: A Pictorial History of the Great Auditorium.* Ocean Grove, N.J.: Ocean Grove Camp Meeting Association, 1994.

Hoyt, Harlowe R. *Town Hall Tonight.* Englewood Cliffs, N.J.: Prentice Hall, 1955.

Izenour, George C. *Theater Design.* New York: McGraw-Hill, 1977.

Jager, Ronald, with Sally Krone. . . . *A Sacred Deposit: The Meetinghouse in Washington, New Hampshire.* Washington, N.H.: Peter E. Randall, 1989.

Johnson, Charlie H., Jr. *The Central City Opera House: A 100-Year History.* Colorado Springs, Colo.: Little London Press, 1980.

Library Theatre. Warren, Pa.: Library Theatre, 1983.

London, Todd. *The Artistic Home.* New York: Theater Communications Group, Inc., 1988.

Lounsbury, Warren C., with Norman Boulanger. *Theatre Backstage from A to Z.* Seattle: University of Washington Press, 1987.

Maddex, Diane, ed. *Landmark Yellow Pages.* Washington, D.C.: Preservation Press, 1990.

Magnuson, Landis K. "New England Ingenuity: The Moveable Opera House Floors of George Gilman Adams." *Theatre Design and Technology,* winter 1992.

Marquee. Quarterly publication of the Theatre Historical Society of America, Chicago, 1969– .

McDermott, Douglas, with Robert K. Sarlos. *The Woodland Opera House.* California Historical Society, n.d.

Mines, Cynthia. *The McPherson Opera House: A Prairie Landmark.* McPherson Opera House Preservation Co., Inc., 1992.

Monette, Clarence J. *The Calumet Theater.* Lake Linden, Mich.: Welden H. Curtain, 1979.

Morrison, Theodore. *Chautauqua: A Center for Education, Religion, and the Arts in America.* Chicago: University of Chicago Press, 1974.

Murray, Robert. *Wheeler Opera House.* Aspen, Colo.: Wheeler Opera House, 1984.

Myers, Denys Peter. *Gaslighting in America: A Guide for Historic Preservation.* Washington, D.C.: U.S. Department of the Interior, 1978.

National List of Historic Buildings. Washington, D.C.: League of Historic American Theatres, 1979, 1987.

National Register of Historic Places. Washington, D.C.: U.S. Department of the Interior, 1976.

Naylor, David. *American Picture Palaces.* New York: Van Nostrand Reinhold, 1981.

———. *Great American Movie Theaters.* Washington, D.C.: Preservation Press, 1987.

Nebraska History. Quarterly publication of the Nebraska State Historical Society, summer 1974.

Nevada Historical Society. *Eureka's Yesterdays.* Reno, Nev.: Nevada Historical Society, 1988.

Patterson, Virginia. *Early History of Haysville and Vermillion Township.* Haysville, Ohio: Haysville Lions Club, 1988.

Pendragon. *Tombstone: The Town Too Tough to Die.* Tempe, Ariz.: Smith-Southwestern, Inc., 1990.

Pickering, Jerry V. *Theater: A History of the Art.* St. Paul, Minn.: West Publishing, 1978.

Pomeranc, Joan. *Fine Arts Building.* Chicago: Commission on Chicago Historical and Architectural Landmarks, 1984.

Provincetown: 250 Years. Provincetown, Mass.: Provincetown Historical Association, Inc., 1977.

Rangstrom, Ture. *Drottningholms Slottsteater*. Sweden, 1985.

Rivenbark, D. Anthony. Essay in *Time, Talent, Tradition*. Wilmington, N.C.: Cape Fear Musuem, 1993.

Sandy, Wilda, with Larry K. Haack. *Stalking Louis Curtiss*. Kansas City, Mo.: Ward Parkway Press, 1991.

Schoenfeld, Mary Margaret, with Grey Hautaluoma, et al. "Curtain Up: New Life for Historic Theaters." Information Series no. 72. Washington, D.C.: National Trust for Historic Preservation, 1993.

Siena, Marcia A. "The History of the Great Southern Theatre." Master's thesis, Ohio State University, 1957.

Southern, Richard. *The Seven Ages of the Theater*. New York: Hill & Wang, 1961.

Southworth, Susan and Michael. *AIA Guide to Boston*. Chester, Conn.: Globe Pequot Press, 1992.

Steenrod, Spencer F. *Stuart's Opera House*. Nelsonville, Ohio: The Nelsonville Tribune, 1978

Talman Federal Savings and Loan. *Restoring the Auditorium*. Chicago: Talman Federal, 1964.

Theater Architecture and Stage Machinery. Denis Diderot with Jean Le Rond d'Alembert, eds. Reprint. New York: Arno Press, 1980.

Theatre Classics. Annual publication of the League of Historic American Theatres. Washington, D.C., 1987–93.

Toft, Carolyn Hewes, Esley Hamilton, and Mary Henderson Gass. *The Way We Came*. St. Louis: Patrice Press, 1991.

Valerio, Joseph M., and Daniel Friedman. *Movie Palaces: Renaissance and Reuse*. New York: Educational Facilities Laboratories Division, Academy for Educational Development, 1982.

Vanderzyl, Madeline G. *The Pella Opera Block 1900–1918*. Pella, Iowa: Pella Opera House, 1990.

Van Hoogstraten, Nicholas. *Lost Broadway Theatres*. New York: Princeton Architectural Press, 1991.

Whiting, Frank M. *Introduction to the Theatre*. 4th ed. New York: Harper & Row, 1978.

Young, Toni. *The Grand Experience*. Watkins Glen, N.Y.: American Life Foundation, 1976.

Zivanovic, Judith K., ed. *Opera Houses of the Midwest*. Publication of the Mid-America Theatre Conference, 1988.

Acknowledgments

Considerable support was given to the authors of this book by the two principal agencies for theater preservation in this country: the League of Historic American Theatres and the Theatre Historical Society of America (THS). Along with the members of both groups, singled out for thanks are their lead operatives in 1995: Mary Margaret Schoenfeld at the former League headquarters in Washington, D.C., and Richard Sklenar at the THS archives in Elmhurst, Illinois.

Additional help came from those individuals working for theaters and related preservation groups around the country. Along with the gratitude expressed to those professionals and volunteers listed here, Joan also wishes to give a special thanks to the hundreds of town clerks who patiently steered her in the right direction to their local theaters. David wants to note the skill and high professional standards of film labs nationwide, with particular thanks to the staffs at Chrome, Inc., in Washington, D.C.; at Ivey-Seright in Seattle, Washington; to Douglas W. Stone and Mammoth Cameras in Irvine, California; and at Donahue Color Services in Wilmington, Delaware, with the lion's share due to Kathleen Donahue and her colleagues. David also sends thanks for Down Under photographic assistance to Merv Gordon and Michael Bennett at the University of Queensland in Brisbane, Australia (in addition to his Ph.D. supervisor, Dr. John P. Macarthur, and department head Michael Keniger, for allowing time off for bookwork).

Individual acknowledgments by state:

ALABAMA: Robert Gamble, Carolyn Hinson, James Kuykendahl, Rusty Myers. ALASKA: Judith Bittner, Russell Sackett. ARIZONA: Burt and Dorothy Devere, Bill Hunley, Jay Ziemann. ARKANSAS: Marjorie Armstrong, Wilson Stiles, Patrick Zollner. CALIFORNIA: Tom D'Attilo, Marta Becket, Mr. Brousard, Tom Carnes, Elaine Edstrom, Rochelle Frazier, Jonathan Fry, Cynthia Howse, Susan Kruzmeyer, Bridget Maley, Paul Matson, Neil Mill, John Miller, Page Pedri, Patricia Perry, Debra J. Ramos, Charles Wallace, Hillsman Wright. COLORADO: Arla Aschermann, Dana Crawford, Leslie Durgin, Rosemary Fedder, Evelyn E. Furman, Felicia Harmon, Dale Heckendorn, Betty Hull, Ellen Ittleson, Rheba Massey, Deborah Woo Moodey, Scott Moore, Robert Murray, Wayne Pleasants, Maureen Robinson, Elaine Scanlon, JoAnn Sims, Mary Sullivan, Andrew R. Thoms, Steve Watkins. CONNECTICUT: David Bartlett, Mary Donohue, F. M. Fay, Susan Frost, Barry Goodkin, John Pike, Michael Price, Bill Reynolds, Steve Sigel, Leo Sochocki, Ann Street, Stuart Ungar, Gilbert A. Wagner, Jr., Jennifer Wislocki. DELAWARE: George Caley, Ellen Davis, Tom English, Patricia Goetz, Joan Larrivee, Rick Neidig, Sara Lu Schwartz. DISTRICT OF COLUMBIA: Jennifer Collins Daly, Susie Farr, Suzanne Ganschinietz, Grey Hautaluoma, Glenn Liner, Jon Radulovich, Jeff Wyatt. FLORIDA: Kathleen Anderson, Rod Layer, Helen Rouse, Tisha Sheldon, Lee Terzis. GEORGIA: Helen C. Alexander, Deborah Arnette, Melvin Hill, Richard Hutto, Clason Kyle, Leonard Myers, Gwen O'Looney, Margaret O'Neil, Sybil Smith, Mary Stakes, Ken Thomas. HAWAII: Lowell Angell, Bill Chapman,

Phyllis Fox, Bill Murtaugh. IDAHO: Eddie Bostie, Karen Bowers, David Crowder, Ann Woodhouse. ILLINOIS: Beth Baranski, Judy Beckes, Sandra Black, Lori Jo Fergle, B. Andrew C. Fowler, Dale Garvey, Dulcie Gilmore, Tom Graham, Jan Link, Colleen Marinich, Richard Maynard, Joe Robinson, Ernie Schuchert, Delmar Stewart, Ann Swallow, Bart Swindall, Meredith Taussig. INDIANA: Michael Breeden, Mary Ann Claesgens, Jon Crisman, Jennie Jengan, Laurene Mykrantz, Suzanne Rollins, Sharon Sadler, A. H. Schumaker, Patricia Sides, Leslie Torok, Reid Williamson, Scott Wood. IOWA: Gilbert Alpers, Don Clark, Robert Fridley, Amy Groskopf, Christine Hanson, John Harris, James Jacobsen, Sandie Nelson, Susan Riedel, Joe Robinson, Bill Stark, John and Mildred White. KANSAS: Jackie Engel, Bernd Foerster, Kelley Goss, Martha Hagedorn-Krass, Margaret Hawley, Donna Lyndeen, Raymond Morris, Charles Sesher, Terry Thibodeau, Joe Vocasek. KENTUCKY: Debbie Cordray, Nancy Farmer, Dick Pardy, Tom Saunders, Phil Weber. LOUISIANA: Richard Freeman, Jonathan Fricker. MAINE: Mott Atherholt, Richard Burns, M. George Carlson, Nancy Dowling, Holly Dumaine, Paul Gagne, Richard Lambert, Renee O'Neil, Jeffrey Quinn, Earl Shettleworth. MARYLAND: Ron Andrews, Robert Pomeroy, Orlando Rideout, Kurt Schmoke, Nancy and Tim. MASSACHUSETTS: Andrew Baker, Robert Bayard, Jayce Beaton, Klaus Bendell, Robert Brien, Regina Curtis, Ann Dumaresq, Craig Edwards, Eve Geller, Richard Gibbons, Thelma Goldberg, Kristen Hennrikus, Raymond Houle, Sondra Katz, Karen Kelley, John Knight, Drew Lydotes, Jerome and Paul Murphy, Pete Patrisco, John Platt, Polly Pierce, Duane Robinson, Edward Sampson, Norma Sandison, Lori Schaefer, R. Schrade, David Scott, Rachel and Io Vanger, Julia White. MICHIGAN: Bob Alexander, Kim Batdorff, Jean Bliss, Bob Christianson, Sue Cone, Joyce Dickinson, Michael Hauser, Russell Lavery, Joann Leal, Patricia Pawlicki, Hildred Peabody, Marilyn Smith, Robert A. Soller, Jim Spittle. MINNESOTA: John Cole, Linnea Engstrom, Mark Gould, Rosina Rittner, Homer Ruby, Marlys Vanderwerf, Ken Wyberg. MISSISSIPPI: Todd Sanders, Elliot Street. MISSOURI: Claire Blackwell, Bill Bruning, Jane Flynn, Ginny Miller, Doug Tatum, Roselle Tyner, John Uzell, Hilda Wallace. MONTANA: Pat Bik, Tim Dringle. NEBRASKA: Densel Fankhauser, Jean Gilkerson, Beth Klosterman, Patricia Phillips, Ray Simmons, Floyd Urtiska. NEVADA: James Chavis, Wally Cuchine, Louis Driggs, Ron James, Lynn Lloyd. NEW HAMPSHIRE: Nancy Cruger, Dale Ford, Albert Garneau, John Goyette, Sally Krone, Nancy Norwalk, Elaine Rayno, Betty Richer, Matthew Thomas, Donald Tirabassi, Linda Ray Wilson. NEW JERSEY: Robert Craig, David Fleming, James Lindemuth, Alan McCracken, Douglas Rauschenberger. NEW MEXICO: Mary Ann Anders, Holm Bursum III, Duke Milovich, Kat Slick, Jean A. Stanley. NEW YORK: Annon Adams, Joanna Baymiller, Jim Boltz, Linda Canzanelli, Gail Caraccilo, Susan Carlton, Linda J. Costa, Richard Erwin, Patrick Fagan, Gino Francesconi, Don Goudreau, Michael Halkias, Hugh Hardy, Alfreda Irwin, Karen Kennedy, Elizabeth Kubany, Peter Lesser, Dede Lieber, Brooks McNamara, Craig Morrison, David Munnell, Karen Noonan, Lisa Reilly, Helen Ringeisen, David Rose, Terry Roth, Ron Samuelson, Julie Schofield, Peter Shaver, Chris Silva, Catherine Spencer, Harold Smith, Julia Stokes, Charles Valenti, Benjie White. NORTH CAROLINA: Susan Mathis, Tony Rivenbark, Jack White. NORTH DAKOTA: Louis Hafermehl, Harlan Hanson, Nick Storhaug. OHIO: Treva Betts, Tom Cinadr, Joe Dapkins, Chuck Edmonson, Irene Gidley, Steve Gordon, Dick Laslow, Gilda Lynch, Susan Mulligan, Don Palm, Virginia Patterson, Michael Roediger, Robert J. Skilliter, Jr., Lora Snow, Rosa Stolz, Paul Sullivan, Michael Young, Phil Zimmerman. OKLAHOMA: Susan Allen, Susan Guthrie, Ralph McCalmont. OREGON: Marian Mulligan, Adrian Owen,

Elizabeth Potter, Fred Reenstjerna. PENNSYLVANIA: Ben Agresti, Brooks Eldrege-Martin, Walter Kidney, Michael Lefevre, Diane Lewis, Clyde Lindsley, Steve Mahofski, Regis McCabe, Gil Peitrzak, Marj Reppert, Diedre Simmons, Maria Sticco, Charles R. Trainter, Deborah Van Horn, Hugh Walsh, Robin Wray. RHODE ISLAND: Antoinette Downing, Linda Hay, Mark Stenning, Fred Williamson. SOUTH CAROLINA: Dan Elswick, Marsha Hewitt, Suzanne M. Mitchell, Summer L. Rutherford, Deborah Smith, Talmadge Tobias. SOUTH DAKOTA: Mike Bedeau, William Ross, Patrick Smith. TENNESSEE: Tom Adkinson, Steve Buchanon, Donna Darwin, Jim Huhta, Allan Jones, Trish McGee, Dr. Van West. TEXAS: Killis Almond, Ned Coleman, Mitzi Douglas, Chester Eitze, Mary Bess Granzin, Clyde Hall, Joann Miller, Maureen Patton, Alexa Powell, Buddy Rau, Laura Rau, Stacey A. Tanet, Esther Trevino, Sherry Ziriax. UTAH: Herb Bossel, Bob Nicholson, Roger Roper. VERMONT: Meg Brazil, Shirley Emilo, Alicia Fisk, Elsa Gilbertson, Gail McNeil, Charles Safford, Martha and Jay Shepperd, Gary Simpson, Marika Szabo, Joanne Waite. VIRGINIA: Debbie Addison, Hugh Miller, Edna Orosick, Margaret Peters, Adam Scher, Debra Yates. WASHINGTON: Kay Austin, Will Conner, Keith McCoy. WEST VIRGINIA: Rodney Collins, Alison Maddex. WISCONSIN: Maggie Foote, Virginia Hirsch, Linda Kraemer, Jeff Miller, Phil Proctor, Rick Railhe, Laura Smalley Reisinger, Patricia Schroeder, Victor and Bessie Stanek, Susan Stare, John Vorndran, Jeffrey and Diane Weaver, Bev and Jack Zavits. WYOMING: Randy Oestman, Nancy Weidel.

On the publishing side, all honor due to Jan Cigliano of Preservation Press/Wiley, for her insightful editing and her wonderful trans-Pacific faxes; to Buckley Jeppson, her predecessor at the Press, for initial interest in the project; and to Amanda L. Miller, Mary Masi, and MaryAlice Yates at the New York City office of John Wiley & Sons, Inc.

Many thoughts as well for those on the home fronts, especially George and Kent Dillon, as well as David K. McHaffey, for the tech support, with thanks to both families and our extended family of friends for years of advice and support.

Index

The League of Historic American Theatres

Founded in 1976, the League of Historic American Theatres (LHAT) is a national membership organization for people who are restoring and operating historic theaters as well as others who support these endeavors in their profession or avocation. One of the primary goals of the League is to identify and document historic theaters. Another is to develop publications to aid those involved with restoring and operating theaters and to sponsor books that increase public awareness and appreciation of historic theaters. These activities support the organization's mission to encourage the rehabilitation and viable operation of historic American theaters as community resources. The League generally defines historic theaters as those that are fifty or more years old, are architecturally significant, and/or have played a prominent role in their community's history or the history of American theatre.

A Note about the Photographs

Most of the photographs for this book were taken over the first half of 1995, as David Naylor traveled more than 40,000 miles to visit just over two hundred theaters. The set of color slides and 6 × 4.5 black-and-white negatives produced by this effort, officially entitled "The LHAT Photodocumentation Project," were intended as a representative sampling of all known operating theaters from the nineteenth century as they appear today. All uncredited illustrations in the book are by David Naylor, drawn from what is now the Dillon Collection of the League of Historic American Theatres.